# MARION NICOLL

## Art and Influences

Christopher Jackson

Glenbow Museum • Calgary, Alberta

The exhibition was organized by the GLENBOW MUSEUM, CALGARY with financial assistance from the CANADA COUNCIL.

This catalogue was made possible through the generous support of the ALBERTA ART FOUNDATION.

## Itinerary

Glenbow Museum, Calgary, April 5, 1986 to June 9, 1986
Edmonton Art Gallery, Edmonton, August 23, 1986 to October 26, 1986

Cover: *Prairie Winter II, Moon in the Morning*, 1961, oil on canvas, Collection of Gerald N. Pencer.

Marion with bear's head, c.1935.

# Contents

# Acknowledgements

This exhibition is presented in recognition of the achievements of Marion Nicoll and the debt that artists and the public in Alberta owe her. Her commitment to art in this province and her artistic integrity has enriched three generations of Albertans who practice artmaking or who simply appreciate visual art. Marion Nicoll's death in 1985 was a loss to us all.

As in all major exhibitions, the end result is due to the efforts and help of many people. I would especially like to thank Janet Mitchell, a long-time friend of Marion Nicoll's and the executrix of her estate, for the time and help she offered me in connection with this project. I also owe special thanks to Rod Green of Masters Gallery in Calgary for the time he took with me to trace the ownership of a number of works in this exhibition that are now in private collections. Their help and patience in this project are deeply appreciated.

My sincere thanks are also extended to Marion Nicoll's friends, former colleagues, and students who agreed to be interviewed for this project and who gave freely of their time: George Wood, John Hall, Eileen Taylor, Clifford Robinson, Stanford Perrot, Illingworth Kerr, Barbara Leighton, ManWoman, Peter Ohler, Stanford Blodgett.

I must also extend special thanks to the private collectors who agreed to make works in their collections available for exhibition, among them: Joan and Dale Simmons, Gerald N. Pencer, Mrs. Moani Moss, Mr. and Mrs. Pierre Hetu, E.D.D. Tavender, Shirley and Peter Savage, Mrs. Betty Anne Graves and Mrs. Eileen Taylor.

In addition, I would like to thank the corporate participants, Chevron Resources Canada Limited, Shell Canada Limited, Gulf Oil Canada Limited, Petro-Canada Limited and Masters Gallery Limited for their involvement in this project.

My special thanks are also offered to Betty Rothwell, registrar of the Alberta Art Foundation for allowing me to view the Foundation's extensive collection of Marion Nicoll's work and for her time and patience in answering my many queries about the works in that collection. I also offer thanks to the curators and registrars of the Art Gallery of Hamilton, the London Regional Art Gallery, the Art Gallery of Windsor, the Winnipeg Art Gallery, the University of Lethbridge Art Gallery, the Nickle Arts Museum, the Ringhouse Gallery, University of Alberta, and the Edmonton Art Gallery for answering my questions and agreeing to lend works to the exhibition.

I also wish to thank Beth Duthie for her excellent editing of the catalogue manuscript, Eugene Ouchi of Stepstone Design for the design of the catalogue, and Maureen Johnson of Walford and Foy for co-ordinating the teletypesetting of the catalogue.

There are a number of people within the Glenbow Museum itself to whom I wish to offer my sincere thanks. I would like to thank John Vollmer, Curator of Fine and Decorative Arts for offering me the opportunity to undertake this exhibition. Assistant Curators Patricia Ainslie and Vincent Varga, provided encouragement and help throughout the organization of the exhibition. I offer my thanks to Ron Marsh, who photographed the majority of works that appear in this catalogue, and to Pam Smith, Daryl Betenia, and Linda Kurtz for their efforts in co-ordinating the numerous loans connected with the exhibition. Rick Budd offered continuing support in connection with the creation of this catalogue. Susan Balfour handled the considerable correspondence generated during the organization of the exhibition. I also wish to thank John Vollmer and Assistant Director Hugh Dempsey for their valuable suggestions and comments on the catalogue manuscript. In addition, the support of the Glenbow Board of Governors and Duncan F. Cameron for this project is gratefully acknowledged.

Further, I would like to thank Tin Ng and the board of the Alberta Art Foundation for their generous financial support of this catalogue and the Canada Council for its support of the exhibition.

Finally, I want to acknowledge a special debt to Dr. Zdenka Volavka, Director of Graduate Studies in Art History, at York University without whose encouragement and support during my graduate studies, I would not have been in a position to undertake this project.

Christopher Jackson
Exhibition Curator
Glenbow Museum

*Prophet*, 1960, oil on canvas.
Cat. no. 12

# MARION NICOLL

## Introduction

Although at the time of her death in March 1985 Marion Nicoll had not taught for nearly twenty years, nor painted for more than a decade, the debt Alberta artists owe her has not been forgotten. Three generations of students were influenced by her. Many younger artists in Calgary who never had the opportunity to study with her are often aware of her career and its importance.

Marion Nicoll was among the first Calgary artists to plunge into abstract art, defying the conservative art establishment and opening a whole new era of artmaking that was more aware of international trends. But the battle to establish abstract art in Alberta was a lonely one, and Nicoll faced resistance from other artists and from the art viewing public. Public recognition came late in her career. She was sixty-seven years old when she was made a member of the Royal Canadian Academy, an honour in which she took great pride. The two most important exhibitions of her work – a retrospective mounted by the Edmonton Art Gallery in 1975, and the 1978 exhibition arranged by her friend and dealer Peter Ohler at the Masters Gallery in Calgary – were organized after Nicoll had virtually ceased making art. Her career was cut short by arthritis, with which she had struggled for more than twenty years. The only important biography on Marion Nicoll was produced in 1978 by J. Brooks Joyner in conjunction with the exhibition at Masters Gallery.

Marion was always a rather unconventional person. Despite being from a strict Presbyterian family, she interrupted her high school studies in Calgary to attend school at St. Joseph's Convent in Red Deer because, as she said, "I wanted to." Among other things she was a member of the first glider club to set up in Calgary. As a teacher and artist she was uncompromising, as a public person she shielded herself from the outside with a tough shell, yet as a friend she was intensely loyal. She was often quick to make assessments of people, and once someone had fallen from her grace she could be stubborn about accepting them back as intimates.

Marion was progressive without being revolutionary. She was not afraid to take a new tack in her art, but she abhorred mindless fashion. Although often criticized, she chose her own path and followed it to its end.

Marion Florence MacKay was born and raised in Calgary. Her father, Robert MacKay was a Scottish immigrant from Thurso, who ultimately became the head of the electrical engineering department for the City of Calgary. Her mother was an American of French and Irish descent whose family had immigrated to Evarts, Alberta.

Marion was the first of her family to pursue a career in art, and her artistic calling showed itself quite early. She remembered that in public school, her class was told to draw a flag. Hers had a ripple in it.[1] Friends, scenes around her home, and the landscape she saw during visits to the nearby countryside, provided Marion with subject matter for her drawings.

Marion in Indian costume, c.1928.

While in high school Marion decided she wanted to study art. R.L. Harvey, the school board's itinerant art instructor, suggested she pursue art as a career, and in fact, Marion never finished high school. At age seventeen her parents sent her to Toronto to study at the Ontario College of Art, where the teaching faculty included Group of Seven painters J.E.H. MacDonald, who served as principal of the school, Franz Johnston and Arthur Lismer. Marion remembered:

> "The works produced by the instructors were interesting, but they were for me not exciting. I accepted the academic training without question. Some of the instructors were painting in a slightly modern manner but they taught in an academic fashion . . . By the way I passed all the work there, and it was pie, there was nothing to it and there were too many people and there wasn't enough personal contact with practicing artists."[2]

Marion studied design with Johnston who was teaching principles that in Marion's words were "definitely older than the stuff that he was painting."[3] She did enjoy the regular weekly dinner meetings during which visiting artists, or members of the Group of Seven, would speak to students. She remembered seeing paintings by Emily Carr, although they did not have much of an impact on her at that point. Besides studying design, Marion also studied batik, a craft she especially enjoyed and practiced throughout her career.

# A Firm Foundation

When Marion returned to Alberta after her second year at the Ontario College of Art, she was anemic and had lost considerable weight. Her mother adamantly refused to allow her to return to Ontario. Earlier that year Marion's younger sister Isobel, who was about to go off to university to study architecture, had died of pneumonia. That was the second death of a child in the Mackay household, a son had died before Marion was born.

Marion was not very pleased at the thought of having to transfer to the Provincial Institute of Technology and Art in Calgary (known as Tech at the time). She admitted being rather haughty about having been to O.C.A., then considered the best art school in the country; but it was at Tech that Nicoll met the first artist who was to have a great impact on her life – A.C. Leighton.

Leighton, who was born in 1901 in Hastings, Sussex, England, was eight years older than Marion, but he was already an accomplished painter with a strong reputation. He had served in the Royal Flying Corps during the World War One and had worked as a designer. In 1929, at twenty-eight, Leighton was the youngest member of the Royal Society of British Artists and took over as the head of the Art Department at Tech following the sudden death of the department's founder Lars Haukeness. Leighton originally came to Canada in 1925 to paint landscape scenes for the Canadian Pacific Railroad and had become the CP's chief commercial artist. His contributions as a teacher are truly profound. He served as head of the Art Department at Tech, and was founder of the Alberta Society of Artists and the summer painting sessions, which eventually became the visual art section of the Banff school of Fine Arts. Between 1929 and 1937 he was the Art Director for the Province of Alberta.

A.C. Leighton, *Floe Lake, Marble Canyon* 1930, water-colour, Collection of the Glenbow Museum, (not included in the exhibition).

Leighton's work was a direct extension of the British watercolour traditions that date back to the eighteenth century and the watercolours of such artists as Paul Sandby. Leighton's watercolours could range from broad, open renditions of landscape to pen and ink or pencil drawings which had been "coloured in" with watercolours. He had full control of his medium and its various ranges, and he was a master of tonal variation and colour control. The British-born painter had a passionate love of the mountains and Canadian landscape. It was a love that he instilled in virtually all his students; it was a passion that would also seize Marion Nicoll.

But if Nicoll was self-assured when she went to Tech to show Leighton her portfolio from O.C.A., she was shocked when Leighton looked at her portfolio and insisted she had not learned how to draw, nor had she any understanding or control of colour. He promptly put Nicoll back in first year. Her feelings of superiority vanished. Unlike some students who would have protested, it is indicative of Marion that she accepted Leighton's criticism. Within four months she had advanced back into third year.

It was also indicative of Leighton's commitment to art that he would not let anyone breeze through his courses. He insisted on discipline and fundamentals. While he felt that artists would have to find their own means of expression, he felt that one could not fully develop as an artist without studying and mastering the basic techniques of art. Leighton was no less harsh in assessing his own work. He is known to have destroyed the majority of the works he painted because they did not meet his standards, and the ones he kept were reviewed annually and culled.

Marion credited Leighton with giving her a firm grasp of the fundamentals of art and an especially thorough understanding of colour. His use of tone and colour, balance between light and dark, warm and cold was exquisite. Leighton once told her that it did not matter what colours she painted something as long as the tone was right and the warmth or coolness of the colour was right.

Marion would say later:

"...Leighton's way of teaching was just as academic as it had been at O.C.A. but he was a totally different sort of person. He saw the possibilities of what was coming and he said that this country would be painted by people who were born here; that he was a visitor...and would never be as close to it as the people who were born in this place, and it would never be painted until somebody here did it..."[4]

Leighton's insistence on inculcating firm technical control was highlighted for Marion by one particular incident. He saw her painting a loose, open landscape scene while she was attending his summer course in Seebe. Unhappy with her technical abandon, he told her to go into the bunkhouse, put a shoe on the floor and paint it so that he could see "the stitching on it." But his openness to new dynamic painting also revealed itself when he took his students into a locked storeroom to show them an Emily Carr exhibition which the head of Tech had banned from exhibition because it was too modern.[5]

Marion responded to this forceful teacher; her early works bear his influence. She produced naturalistic landscapes, clearly setting out the structure of the scene and painted in controlled colours which at times verge on monochrome. Leighton obviously saw potential in Marion's work. In 1931, while she was still a student, he made her an instructor at Tech. He also invited her to his summer courses at Seebe. Even after Leighton left Tech due to ill health, Marion stayed in touch with him. Much later, in the 1960s, after Marion had returned from New York and was painting abstracts, she continued to bring paintings to his studio for critiques and discussions.[6]

Detail: *On the Ghost*, 1941, from sketchbook, pencil on paper.
Cat. no. 70

For more than twenty years her watercolours of the landscape in southern Alberta bore the stamp of his teaching. Marion did not re-create the hot, blazing colours of the Group of Seven members that she studied under in Toronto, nor the rich swirling forms of the British Columbia forest as depicted by Emily Carr. She chose to paint in the colours of her surrounding landscape. Her colours were never intense, but conveyed completely the tones of rock mountain and grassy prairie.

Immediately after graduating, Marion became a craft instructor in Tech's Art Department. In the face of the Depression, teaching provided her with an income which allowed her to pursue an artistic career. She certainly could not have hoped to support herself by painting alone. In fact, she never had the luxury of doing so.

In 1933, Henry Glyde was named the director of the Art Department at Tech after Leighton's health failed. Glyde, another Englishman, had worked in Leighton's studio in Britain, and Leighton had brought him to Canada to teach. Marion never developed a particularly close relationship to him. Glyde had very different ideas on developing the artistic community from Marion's beloved teacher. He felt that more British artists should be brought in to teach young Albertans. In his art history classes he often held British artists up as role models. It was a view that did not sit well with home-grown artists who

*October*, 1956, watercolour.
Cat. no. 43

were coming into their own, and it certainly did not fit the vision that Leighton had for the development of art in the region.

In 1937, Marion took a one-year leave from her teaching post at Tech so that she could study design at the London County Council School of Art and Crafts. While in London, Marion took advantage of both the school and the richness of the city. In a taped interview in the Glenbow Archives, Marion recounted how she regularly visited the major museums in London: the British Museum, the National Gallery, and the Tait.[7] She sketched continually and made several trips around the the United Kingdom. Her sketchbooks are filled with charming renditions of old towns and buildings, as well as drawings of pottery and furniture design which she studied at school. Marion also visited Norway, Sweden, and Denmark. Her studies and travels in 1937 and 1938 exposed her not only to the works of old masters, but also to some of the more progressive art being produced in Europe at the time. No doubt the work she saw planted the seed of discontent that would ultimately lead her to investigate abstraction.

Shortly after her return to Calgary in 1938, Marion's personal life also changed. In the early 1930s she had met James McLaren Nicoll, a civil engineer, poet and artist, at a meeting of the Calgary Sketch Club. In 1940, she married Jim Nicoll. Despite the fact that both were painters, their work could hardly be more dissimilar. Jim did, however, provide Marion with an emotional support that no doubt allowed her to continue her development over the next forty years.[8]

11

# A New Path Opens

Jock and Barbara Macdonald, Marion and Macdonald's dog Watchie, c.1946.

At thirty-five, Marion felt that she had acquired the requisite technique from her firm academic training under Leighton; she had learned to handle the tools of art and had a sound knowledge of the principles of design. But conceptually she was dissatisfied with her painting. Marion would say later that she felt compelled to produce because she had been trained as an artist, not because she received any satisfaction from her work during the period.[9] The naturalistic style she inherited from Leighton was wearing thin, and she was looking for something new to get her out of the quandary in which she found herself. Jock Macdonald provided the the answer — automatic drawing.

Marion Nicoll first met Jock Macdonald in 1946 after he had come to Tech to take over the Art Department from Glyde, who had left Calgary to become head of the Art Department at the University of Alberta in Edmonton. Macdonald

himself had become interested in automatics in the early 1940s through Grace Pailthorpe, a British psychologist and artist whom he met in Vancouver where she was lecturing on automatic painting.[10]

Automatic painting was born of the French Surrealist movement founded by poet Andre Breton and grew initially from Freudian psychology. It was, in part, an anti-mechanistic movement prompted by the carnage of World War One. Automatism sought to tap the unconscious and bring those feelings and visions to surface. These submerged feelings and forms, suppressed by the conscious civilized mind, were felt to be aspects of reality hitherto unexplored. The reality of which automatistes spoke was not the reality of the perceptual world, but rather the reality of the inner world of the human mind. Surrealism placed great store in dream and primordial images.

Automatism was popular in Europe in the early part of the twentieth century, just as the new science of psychiatry and its study of madness and mental disorder became a subject of widespread debate. Some scientists and many artists began to believe that madness might simply be another form of reality to that which the average person perceived. Visually, of course, it allowed artists who had been exploring the imagery of non-literate cultures to press further in their attempts to create an imagery which was free from bourgeois sentiment. Artists found automatic painting, drawing and writing liberating because they allowed them to break with conventions that had been established over centuries of European art. The artists defended their work against criticism by stressing that they were depicting an interior, rather than an exterior reality, that explored the human subconscious and revealed essential truths about human beings, rather than the perceptual truths of the eye.

Marion had become aware of automatic painting in Canada through the magazine, *Canadian Art*, which carried articles on *Les Automatistes*, the circle of Quebec artists founded by Paul Emile Bourduas and Jean-Paul Riopelle. She was fascinated by their work. When she met Macdonald and learned that he was doing automatic paintings and drawings, she:

"...asked Jock about the things he was doing, how he reached these strange different images...there were queer ones of fish, and there'd be queer-looking gods. He said, 'You take a pencil, you are in a quiet place, you put the pencil on the paper and you sit there and wait until your hand moves of its own accord. You do that every day, you date it, even put down the time of day and you do it steadily, don't miss a day — you keep on doing it. It will happen without any effort on your part.'"[11]

J.W.G. Macdonald, *Russian Fantasy*, 1946, watercolour and ink on paper, 25.7 x 35.7 cm, Collection of the Art Gallery of Ontario, Toronto, Purchase, Peter Larkin Foundation, 1962. (not included in the exhibition).

*Untitled*, April 1948, automatic watercolour. Cat. no. 33

*Migration*, 1964, oil on canvas.
Cat. no. 22

The effect of automatic drawing on Nicoll was immediate and profound. By her own account, Nicoll virtually ceased to paint anything else and concentrated on automatics. She divided her energies between working on automatics and teaching crafts and design.[12]

Much later, Marion's husband Jim told her dealer, Peter Ohler, that the change in Marion was startling. He said he seemed to be living with a new person with a new and frightening strength to create images rather than photocopies of the landscape.

Marion followed a daily regimen of doing automatics between 1946 and 1957, and continued to do them sporadically until the end of her career, but she maintained that they were never destined for exhibition.

"...it's strictly a studio exercise – it's the scales. I'm beginning to think that it can be an art form. Because I'm trained [that] what I turn out can be art, can be considered an art object."[13]

From the outset, Marion seized upon automatic drawing as a way to "beat a path through the undergrowth" and reach something more essential in her art. Marion drew from Carl Jung's writings and felt that no human experience is forgotten, no matter how trivial it may seem to the conscious mind.[14]

She believed these memories are stored in the subconscious and rise to the surface only during dream-like states or during those unconscious periods such as when she was doing automatics. These concepts drawn ultimately from Jung were quite likely reinforced by Macdonald.

Marion went through an eleven-year gestation period. Outwardly, she concentrated on crafts and teaching. Inwardly, she explored the amazing wealth of the subconscious imagery which sprang from her pen and brush. All her artistic strength and attention seemed to be centred on these psychic adventures which took her over completely.

For an artist who had hitherto been schooled in academic correctness and disciplined technique, the new forms, at first tentative and then flowing, must have been frightening. Up to that point, Marion had looked to the natural world for her forms and subject matter, recreating what she perceived with her eye. Now she was floating free on her subconscious. Being free from conscious control allowed her to take advantage of fortuitous shapes and configurations of form, odd combinations of line and shape, and random composition.

Marion remained disciplined and followed Macdonald's directions strictly. Page upon page of her sketchbooks are filled with automatics, many dated by day, sometimes by year and time as well. Some of these automatics seem to be random scribbles which are little more than the "scales" as Nicoll described them. Others, however, are visual delights which stand quite confidently as independent works of art. Because Marion was not doing these automatic drawings for exhibition, there could be no failures, simply more or less fruitful explorations. Her automatics are open and fluid, unlike Macdonald's which were often re-worked for exhibition.

As Marion became more acquainted and confident with the technique, she became more and more interested in the sources of these strange shapes and images she was producing. It became clear to her that she was producing images that responded to their own inner logic and compositional necessities rather than to some external paradigm of correctness.

The automatics inexorably pushed Marion away from the perceptual world and into the realm of conceptual realities as she tried to digest the meanings and sources of these works. She began to see extensions of form and association in the fragments of nature that appeared in her work. Her work would become synedochal rather than re-creative. The barriers were

J.W.G. Macdonald, *Winter*, 1938, oil on canvas, Art Gallery of Ontario, Toronto, gift of Miss Jessie A.B. Staunton in memory of her parents, Mr. and Mrs. V.C. Staunton, (not included in the exhibition).

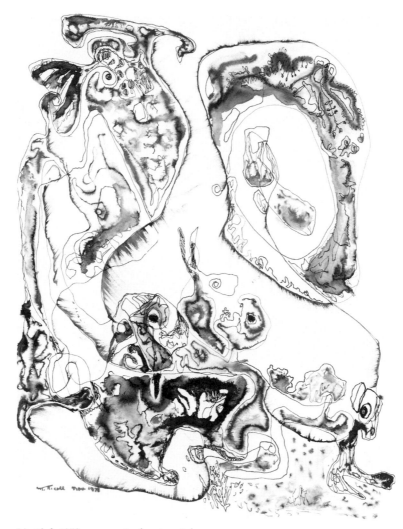

*Untitled*, 1978, automatic drawing, ink on paper.
Cat. no. 76

being broken down; she began to put her faith more fully in intuitive connections rather than in the safety in mimetic form.

The automatics are extremely difficult to explain. The strange beasts, configurations and juxtapositions are not the willed and conscious productions of an artist but rather unconscious and undirected, and do not conform to artistic conventions. It is doubtful that Marion herself "understood" them in the way we generally talk of understanding art. Marion was more concerned and fascinated with the enigmas they presented as she tried to define and trace their source.

Nicoll gained several advantages from automatic drawing. Firstly, she was freed of convention and correctness. Secondly, it allowed her to separate the conceptual from the perceptual, and thirdly, the automatics familiarized her with accidental relationships of line and form. While there are very few instances of direct visual relationships between the automatics and her later abstract work, there can be no doubt that the automatics broke down her academic prejudices and allowed her to make use of abstract forms.

16

The mystery and foreboding which appeared in her automatics made their way into some of the more traditional works Marion painted during this period. *Badlands at Eladesor* (Cat. no. 40), a watercolour painted in 1953, and *Graveyard and Hoodoos* (Cat. no. 4), an oil painted in 1955, both have a slightly ominous undertone. Each is painted in unpretty colours with a black accenting. The expressiveness of the two works hints at the exploration Marion was carrying on privately in her automatics.

In the 1930s, Macdonald began working on what he called "modalities" in an attempt to pursue a more modern, abstract style. These modalities were not pure abstraction, but extensions of natural forms or idioms of nature which formed a type of visual shorthand, evoking fundamental sensations and emotional associations connected with his subject. He attempted not so much to depict a subject, as to re-create a concept in paint. The subjects of his paintings in the 1930s tend towards seasons, and phenomena. For example, in a painting called *Rain*, (1938) he attempted to capture what is common to the concept of all rainstorms. Again in a painting *Flight*, (1939) it was the essential element of all flight he wished to depict.[15]

Nicoll's work reflects a similar interest. Although visually dissimilar, such paintings as *Migration* (Cat. no. 22) or *Spring* (Cat. no. 8) go beyond mere manipulation of visual forms to attempt a synthesis of form, association and sensation; a meld of perceptual realities with conceptual realities.

The concepts of essential form, the primordial and the archetypal became extremely important to Marion later in the 1960s, when she wholeheartedly committed herself to abstraction. Such paintings as *January 1969*, (Cat. no. 27); *Ritual II*, 1962, (Cat. no. 20); *Eclipse*, 1962, (Cat. no. 21) and *Sundogs*, 1967, (Cat. no. 24) which are elemental and monumental in conception, bear witness to her concern.

*The Model with Green Towel*, 1958, watercolour. Cat. no. 45

# The Chrysalis Cracks: Emma Lake

Marion's visit to the Emma Lake workshop conducted by Will Barnet in 1957 is considered by most observers to be the turning point in her move from naturalistic to abstract painting. From that point on, Marion completely abandoned naturalism. Neither she nor the Calgary artists who accompanied her to Emma Lake suspected that she would stride into abstract art so easily. Illingworth Kerr, Stanford Perrot, and Stan Blodgett all were aware of Marion's experimentation with automatic drawing, but the ease with which she moved into abstraction must have been a bit of a surprise.[16] Certainly Marion herself felt as if the change in her work was coming without being bidden.

". . . Barnet had us drawing and we had two or three Indians posing. I worked in watercolour and my hand shook. I just sat there and shook with what

was happening. Nothing had been said about how to approach the problem, only that we were to try and get the essence of the figure. Barnet had his own special way of setting up a pose, putting the figure in a certain position and then extending it with colour pieces, a tilted mirror, a chair, a stack of books, something, so that our eyes expanded away from the figure. Well, this became a totem, an up-and-down thing, with the figure built around that, and I did a dozen, trying to get exactly what I wanted . . . each one became more and more abstract."[17]

Barnet's manner of teaching was something that several of the Calgary artists who attended the course had not expected. Stan Blodgett remembers that he was expecting to see and paint new landscape which he had not encountered up to that time. Instead, all the painting was done indoors in a studio filled with students, and the figure, rather than landscape, was the subject. Barnet, who was teaching at the Art Students League in New York, was very sure of what and how he wanted to teach and the location of the classes mattered little to him.[18]

Barnet had initially been a printmaker but later took up painting. By the 1940s he began to paint abstractions. His style was ultimately derived from a type of figurative Cubism. Inexorably, however, he moved towards a purer hard-edged style of abstraction. In the late 1950s, he began to abandon that style for a renewed figurative style, although his later work clearly reflects his abstract period. It seems that he and Marion met at the zenith of his interest in pure abstraction. He would move back to a more figurative style, while she would continue to paint abstractions.

Marion responded quickly to his method and Barnet's approach made her transition easy and natural. As Brooks Joyner wrote:

"For Marion, the transformation of her painterly sensibilities after Emma Lake are dramatic and complete. The visionary symbolist and the structural neo-classicist merge in her paintings after 1958. This visual rebirth was attended by a new enthusiasm reminiscent of her early growth. She was in pursuit of a new iconography and spatiality."[19]

Marion had originally gone to Emma Lake to study printmaking under Barnet, but the printmaking supplies never arrived, and Barnet had the class under his direction working in watercolour as a substitute. Barnet was the catalyst who opened a new path for Marion and provided support and encouragement for her new direction. At home in Calgary, the general climate was definitely not sympathetic to abstract art, and all signs of it were viciously attacked. Even artists such as Max Bates and Leroy Stevenson, neither of whom were abstract artists, were attacked as being too modern.[20]

Stan Blodgett said the forty-six-year-old Nicoll seemed like a young student again, eager and enthusiastic. She would continually ask Barnet for advice about the placement of forms and the composition of her work.[21]

Marion knew something of Barnet before she went to Emma Lake. Perrot had studied under him in 1954 and had discussed his work with Marion. Barnet was a strong and persuasive teacher. Blodgett remembers that each night Barnet would give a slide lecture about artists he felt were worth studying. Illingworth Kerr reviewed Barnet's lectures in *Highlights*, the Alberta Society of Artists magazine, in the spring of 1958.

"Will Barnet's principal message, delivered in his evening talks . . .was an examination of traditional and modern works which had an essentially classic basis of form and structure – Ingres, Vermeer, etc. Dribble painters like Jackson Pollock, horrific painters like Francis Bacon, bizarre painters like Blume were flushed down the drain. Perhaps Gorky rose as high as any among the moderns. Purity of form and colour ousted the theatrical and the whimsical. In a day of "experiment" Barnet decries the word."[22]

This interest in the old masters and rejection of the gestural and emotional directness of abstract expressionism in favour of a more controlled, rational approach to painting struck a chord in Marion.

Barnet's own work dealt with the under-lying order of its subject. His forms were flat and unmodelled; like cut-outs, carefully enclosed by line or edge, each area with its own discrete colour. Marion adopted this style and began to build on it. Both Barnet and Marion, however, always claimed a link between their work and the natural world.

Marion was so struck by Barnet and his teaching that she decided to continue her studies with him at the Art Students League in New York the following year. The decision to go to New York was a courageous one on Marion's part. She would be stepping into a totally different world. Financially, she would have to forego the security of her teaching income, which was crucial to Jim and her. In fact, her finances were so poor that she was forced to have a yard sale of her earlier works to help supplement her travelling funds. Many of her early watercolours were sold for the price of $5 each.[23]

Marion and Jim Nicoll on Calgary street, c.1950.

## Seeing with New Eyes

Marion's move to New York was the most important decision of her artistic life. Her studies with Barnet convinced her that she should paint abstractions, and that moving to New York would place her in a milieu in which that goal was attainable. It also provided Marion with the opportunity to soak up many international influences and to see the newest trends in art first-hand.

One of her first paintings made under Barnet's direct influence in New York was *East River*, 1958. The painting was Marion's first stride into abstracting a scene from around her and translating that abstraction into oil. In this painting Marion attempted to synthesize a number of elements: the Hudson River, the bridge over it, and the surrounding cityscape. Her awareness of the structure of a scene is evident. The canvas is divided, with the left side dealing primarily with the water of the river and the bridge, while the right side, slightly less than half the area of the canvas, is reserved for the cityscape. Small vertical rectangles of colour represent buildings; they sit side by side and there is slight recession. However, there is a central vertical element which not only divides the canvas into two parts but also strengthens the vertical rectangles. This vertical element also mitigates the strong horizontal form at the top portion of the canvas formed by the bridge itself and the roadway leading from it, creating a subliminal balance of forms. Marion's colours are subdued and act as unifiers. Similar colours or tonal values are repeated over the face of the canvas. The closeness of these values tends to flatten the scene, and one reads it up and down rather than back into space.

In the final analysis, however, Marion felt that *East River* was a failure.

> "I should have destroyed it. But that's where it started. I found myself taking deep breaths — oh, boy — just like that. It stank, and there were all those crimes and everything, but that was a beautiful city. There was a challenge in the air. . .I worked hard. . .I was so full of ideas I couldn't get them all out."[24]

But Marion forced herself to work hard. By November she wrote to her friend Jean Johnston in Calgary to tell her of her progress and reported that she had completed seventeen canvases in eight weeks of work. She felt her work was getting better all the time and noted a change to "better colour and much simpler imagery."[25] Barnet seemed pleased with her work and used it as an example for other students in his class. Marion in fact felt that she was Barnet's pet student, a suggestion that most pleased her.

Marion's letters from New York to friends at home in Calgary describe her invitations to dinner, her trips to the theatre with Jim, and the whirlwind of people she was introduced to by Barnet. He had become as much a friend as a teacher. But she was aware that New York could turn an artist's head and keep her from doing what she had come to do — paint. Marion generally managed to resist distraction and established a routine.

"Barnet's class at the League works from 9 to 12:30 every morning. Then I rush home to make lunch and there is my easel with three big north windows and all the time in the world. Sometimes we go out to a concert or to see something we haven't seen (there is still plenty we haven't got around to yet).

"My class at the League has about six serious painters and a dozen others. We have a life model in the same pose for a week at a time, posed and arranged by Barnet on Mondays. He is there two full mornings a week and the rest of the time there is a monitor. People come and go as they wish. There is a general coffee break at 10:30 – you should see the cafeteria, full of young, old, bearded, smocked, levied, clean and dirty artists and models draped in old bits of scarf or sheet walking around. . ."[26]

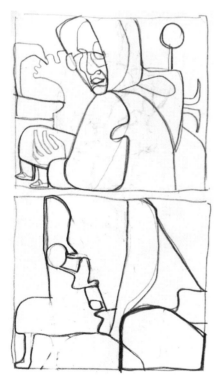

From sketchbook, c.1959, pencil on paper.
Cat. no. 71

By March of 1959 she had amassed about fifty paintings and was taking up to four at a time to Barnet's class for criticism.

Of course, Marion and Jim took time to look at what was going on in the New York galleries. While Marion certainly loved New York, she was aware that it was also the centre of "hype" as well as substance.

". . . we went to the Parke-Bernet gallery, showing the Kirkeby collection of modern masters, going on sale (auction) Wednesday night. It is a much advertised collection and is expected to sell in the millions. There were Modiglianis, Cezannes, Utrillos, Matisses, Dufys and heavens knows what. You'd expect a thrilling show, wouldn't you? It wasn't – every picture but one of the Modiglianis was a fourth rate stinker. We came away depressed and disgusted. Saw the Guggenheim award winners to-day and they didn't make us feel any better."[27]

Marion maintained a healthy skepticism about some of the art she saw. She felt that there were a few sincere artists in New York, among them Hans Hofmann, Jackson Pollock and Mark Rothko. They were breaking new ground; lamentably, they were also attracting a number of imitators and pretenders.

She also found that she was re-evaluating the works of some painters whose work she had seen previously – Pollock, for instance. She had seen reproductions of his work and had not liked it very much, but when she actually saw the paintings, the artist's accomplishment rose dramatically in her estimation. In fact, Pollock's drip paintings may have had special significance for Marion in that they reinforced her own experience with the automatic painting which had given her an entree into abstract painting.

Other artists made an impact on Marion.

"I saw a retrospective exhibition of Miró and I came out of there absolutely drunk, just drunk. There were rooms full of it. . . .You could feel the way he changes. . .the boy throwing the rock on the beach with that funny foot, and the sand and the coloured ball and the dots. I was just delirious when I came out of there, but he was just somebody whose work I liked."[28]

Despite Marion's respect for painters such as Hofmann and Pollock, she was not directly influenced by their styles. She was earnestly independent. In a letter to Jean Johnston, who had compared another artist's work to Marion's, she explained her working method and ideas:

*Model and Reflection*, 1960, oil on canvas.
Cat. no. 10

Will Barnet, *Male and Female*, 1954, oil on canvas, 101.6 x 81.3 cm, Whitney Museum of American Art, New York, anonymous gift through the Federation of Modern Painters and Sculptors, Inc (not included in the exhibition).

*God out of the Night*, 1959, encaustic on board. Cat. no. 29

"Madame, you insult me. That thing you described . . . is 'abstract expressionism' which is anathema to a 'classical abstractionist' such as myself. I start with something — the model — the street we live in, the newsstand at the corner and struggle with the thing, drawing it, trying to find the skeleton that is there. I do this 24 hours a day. I dream it, eat it and agonize over it. (Jim says he feels like pacing the floor and then handing out cigars every time I begin a new subject and carry it through to a finished canvas.) Sometimes it happens easily and two or three canvases result without too much agony . . . but usually it is damned hard work with mistakes barring the way. You have to fight your way through the underbrush with every painting."[29]

In New York Marion felt challenged as a painter, and as she met those challenges, she felt a growing belief in herself and her art. Under Barnet's tutelage, she was not only seeing current art with new eyes but also the work of old masters, to whom he continually referred. Others noticed her as well. She was offered a post teaching at Cooper Union, the design museum, and no less an artistic giant than Barnett Newman suggested that she stay in New York.

The prospect of returning home wrenched Marion. She was well aware that she would not be readily accepted. But she could not stay. A sense of duty to the art school which had given her time off to study in New York and the fact that Jim despised the city and wanted to return to Calgary forced her hand. Marion said later that had she been alone she might have stayed in New York.

The decision to return to Calgary was mitigated by the award of a $2,000 Canada Council grant which enabled Jim and her to go to Spain, Portugal and Sicily. She wrote: "If I had to return to Calgary straight from here instead of having the glow of Italy in front of me I'd cut my throat and bleed messily from here to Times Square."[30]

Marion arranged to send her New York work home and took only small canvases with her to the Mediterranean. On April 25, 1959 Marion and Jim Nicoll boarded the ocean liner *Independence* and sailed for Europe.

# A Style is Formed

Marion had been to Europe before, but that was a very different experience from southern Europe and the Mediterranean in the spring of 1959. The Nicolls were to stay for only two and a half months, but it was to be an extremely important period.

They travelled from New York to Sicily by ship and took lodgings near Taormina on Sicily's west coast. Marion was enchanted and enthralled by the history of Sicily. The pace of life, especially after New York, was much slower. The fishermen still maintained the superstitions of preceding generations, fishing offshore in small brightly coloured boats bearing protective eyes on their prows to ward off evil spirits. The natural rhythms of sea and work provided the clock and the timetable in Sicily.

Marion wrote to Jean Johnston:
"Got a small book on this district and its history is fascinating. First the Greeks in 800 B.C. – they landed and set up their first city right here (Naxos)...
I usually waken at 4 in the morning and watch the fishermen going out from our balcony and I'm up at 7 when they come back. It's a wonderful life...It's heavenly to go to sleep to the sound of the sea.
Taormina is fun to visit, crooked narrow streets with lush flowers and vines and cobbles and steps and traces of the conquerors of the past centuries – Greek, Roman, Saracen, Spanish, French and Italian. Christian churches were built on the old Greek temples and the columns still show in places..."[31]

Marion's sketchbooks of the time are filled with drawings of the towns and villages in the area, with their ancient architecture, their fishing boats and Roman bridges. She was drawn to Sicily as a physical document and record of centuries. Later Marion would paint *Ancient Wall*, 1962 (Cat. no. 17), which was inspired by an old wall with Roman, Saracen and peasant brick work which she felt read like a book. The resulting painting is divided up into small sections obviously drawn from the wall's brickwork. Each "brick" is marked with what looks like a series of runic symbols or hieroglyphs. While these forms and symbols actually say nothing, they appear to hold some silent message, and variations on them would later appear in other paintings.[32]

Sketch for *Sicily II, Ulysses Beach*, sketchbook page, 1959. Cat. no. 71

After their stay in Sicily, the Nicolls made a whirlwind tour of Rome, Ravenna, Venice and Florence before departing for two weeks in Spain. Then it was on to Lisbon before returning to North America. Their time was taken up with trips to museums to see the famous works of Renaissance and Mannerist masters. In Italy, Marion and Jim had visited Assisi to look at the works of Giotto and Cimabue, and in Spain, they travelled to Toledo and marvelled at the work of El Greco. She was seeing first-hand the works of so many painters that Barnet had referred to in his classes.

*The Bird's Nest*, 1948, oil on canvas.
Cat. no. 2

*Sicilia III, Fishing Boats*, 1959,
oil on canvas.
Cat. no. 7

24

*Spring*, 1959, oil on canvas.
Cat. no. 8

Marion in her studio, c.1963.

# In Place and Time

Marion's painting continued to mature after her return from Europe. Her forms became more simplified and her themes seemed to become more timeless and monumental. The visual vocabulary she had originally absorbed from Barnet became her own — simple, classical and enduring. Unlike some of her New York paintings, *Self Portrait* (Cat. no. 9), 1959, for instance, which are made up of a multiplicity of elements, she began to reduce the number of elements in her post-European paintings.

The period between Marion's return to Calgary in the late summer of 1959 and the effective end of her painting career in 1971 was one of intense activity. She returned to teaching with renewed vigour, and students of the time noticed an almost missionary zeal in discussions of abstract painting.[33]

On her return to Calgary, Marion re-painted several of her New York canvases and many of the works she had originally done in small scale in Europe. The Italian and Spanish paintings were worked up to larger pieces. She continued to paint the urban subjects she had first taken up in New York, but increasingly her work during the period became centred around landscape and seasonal phenomena. It is during this time that she painted such works as *Prairie Winter II — Moon in the Morning*, 1961 (Cat. no. 15), *East from the Mountains*, 1961 (Cat. no. 14), *Eclipse*, 1962, *Migration*, 1964, *Sundogs*, 1967, and her

series on months and seasons, such as *Spring*, 1963, and *January*, 1969. The figure, which had so occupied her while she was in New York, virtually disappeared from her major canvases. There are a few examples, *Ritual II*, 1962, *Pregnant Woman*, 1963, but these are very different from her work from the model. They are concerned with the common events shared in virtually all women's lives, the rites of passage, rather than events in a particular woman's life.

Marion's mature work exhibits a personal *melange* of Leighton's interest in landscape, Macdonald's interest in the essence of nature and the eternal, and Barnet's abstract forms. But these works — while the influences are readily discernible in form, theme and philosophical approach — are not derivative pastiches, rather they are Nicoll's own extension of her influences, a personal style of her own creation. Her detractors, and they did exist in some numbers, superficially viewed her as a "little Will Barnet"; Clement Greenberg, the much vaunted American formalist critic of the day, commented that he saw the "helpful influence of Will Barnet" in her work.[34] That seemed to buttress her detractors' views. But such a view is born of a fundamental, and perhaps willful, misunderstanding of what Nicoll was doing. Marion's work was her own. While the forms might be ultimately derived from Barnet and other late generation Cubists, her intent and her themes were quite different. She developed a style laden with personal, symbolic elements which begin to recur in her work: the often present solar-lunar disc which represents, at different times, the actual heavenly bodies or a symbol of the seasons; her use of positive and negative shapes to indicate changes in time and season. Marion also used a "tunnel-like" form, as in *Madrid II, Night and Day* (Cat. no. 13), within which there is the potential for the sun-moon to move, representing the passage of time. Her interlocking forms and use of colour became increasingly personal. Marion's painting became more and more spare, all non-essentials were gradually eliminated until she had lain bare the underlying structure of her subject, its universal components.

Brooks Joyner suggests that Marion's landscapes became mythical or allegorical; that her iconography became more personal and expressed the archetypal rites of passage in contemporary society.[35]

Marion had begun to suffer from arthritis as early as 1950 and had mentioned suffering from it while she was in New York. By 1965 it had grown so bad that she was forced to retire from A.C.A. In 1970, she had an operation to relieve her pain, but by that time she had virtually ceased to paint. She was working against time and she knew it. For someone as committed and creative as Marion Nicoll, the hardship, both physical and psychological, was acute. At one point, in a near desperate at-

*Bowness Road, 2 a.m.*, 1963, oil on canvas.
Cat. no. 19

tempt to stave off the advance of her arthritis, Marion turned to a clinic which apparently used unconventional treatments. She wrote brief accounts in her notebook of how she felt after the series of treatments:

"June 1. I'm home now. I've wept with hysterical relief and thanks for a miracle. I'm free of pain. Tomorrow at 10 a.m. second treatment. I *can't believe it.*

June 2. Second treatment — not as rough as the first. Got up this morning, completely free of pain. The deepest best *drug free* sleep I've had for months . . . I feel so well and so *clearminded.* Now I can paint. God."[36]

The treatments, which lasted a month, ultimately failed to stem the development of her arthritis. She kept painting as long as possible, but arthritis finally ended her career.

Once it became clear that painting was becoming too difficult for Marion, she began to turn increasingly to print-making as an outlet. Many of her prints were based on paintings which she had already executed. The clay process was used most often because the medium was easy to handle, although she also did cardboard, plasticine prints and woodcuts as well. Many of these prints are beautiful and subtle variations·of the themes she re-worked from paintings.[37]

During the 1960s, Marion began to exhibit more regularly, often with favourable critical reviews. Will Barnet in New York was pleased with the news and wrote to her:

". . . all your exhibiting is going to add up one day and you will awake one morning as queen of the Canadian painting world. Of course, this is only the first step and there are many other thrones awaiting you."[38]

*Self Portrait*, 1959, oil on canvas.
Cat. no. 9

*Ancient Wall*, 1962, oil on canvas.
Cat. no. 17

Marion's works, paintings and prints, appeared in group exhibitions in Chicago, Ottawa and Europe, and she had solo exhibitions in Edmonton, Toronto and Winnipeg. Greenberg, who was doing an assessment of Canadian art for the magazine *Canadian Art* in 1963, wrote that her work was "among the best in oil and in watercolour" that he saw in Canada.[39] In 1965, Ken Winters wrote a review of her work for the *Winnipeg Free Press* and said:

> "Perhaps the special validity for us in [Mrs.] Nicoll's 14 severe and monumental gestures in paint is something more parochial and more personal than her splendid reconciliation of the abstract and the elemental. To be sure she says basic things with a minimum of fuss, and this is the source of the dignity and honesty of her work. But for Canadians it also will be significant that she says things in a particularly Canadian voice... her colours have their source in the unsentimental colours of the fruits of our native earth; her thoughts have the stern, unostentatious sense that we like to believe is the best characteristic of the workings of our national mind."[40]

In a review of her work exhibited in Chicago, Edward Barry of the *Chicago Tribune* wrote that: "Marion Nicoll seeks to evoke, but not to literally describe, the procession of the seasons across the western provinces of Canada."[41]

Don Anderson, who wrote a review of a group show at the Vincent Price Sears Gallery in Chicago which included Marion's work, stated, "The most powerful painter of the four is Marion Nicoll. Her compositions are strong and simplified to dominant division of space and form. One entitled *Pregnant Woman* translates with its design pattern a complete feeling of weight and size to be concerned with in the circle-based composition."[42]

The reviews from Calgary tended not to discuss her art, except to note what others had said. More often the discussion revolved around the fact that she was a teacher or that she had a penchant for smoking cigarillos. While not antagonistic, the reviewers often tended to be more restrained in their enthusiasm. This cool response to Marion's work over the years had troubled her. But she received support from her friends and teachers, most notably Macdonald and Barnet, in the face of what she perceived as resistance to her work. Barnet often wrote to Marion, lamenting the resistance and lack of response and understanding of her work at home and urged her to be courageous and to continue painting "as she must."[43]

In the 1960s Marion began to get commissions. She designed a playground in Calgary and one for the Y.W.C.A. in New York. She was also asked to design a wall for a campground near Tilley, Alberta, on the Trans-Canada Highway. However, one commission into which Marion truly put a great deal of energy ended in disillusion. A private collector in Edmonton commissioned her to paint a triptych of immense size (approximately nine feet by twelve feet overall). Marion presented the collector with drawings and sketches of the work, and it took her more than a year to complete the painting itself. Marion put a great deal of money as well as time into the project and the physical cost was enormous. However, when Marion finally transported the work to Edmonton, the collector backed out of the commission. Dejected and furious, Marion returned the work to Calgary, where the massive *Journey to the Mountains and Return*, 1968-1969, was eventually placed in the library lobby of the University of Calgary.

Detail: *Red Spring*, 1961, felt pen and ink.
Cat. no. 73

*Guaycura IV, Our Lady of La Paz,*
1966, oil on canvas.
Cat. no. 23

*Ritual II*, 1963, oil on canvas.
Cat. no. 20

*Alarum*, 1976, clay print.
Cat. no. 61

*Friendly Encounter*,
no date, mixed media.
Cat. no. 83

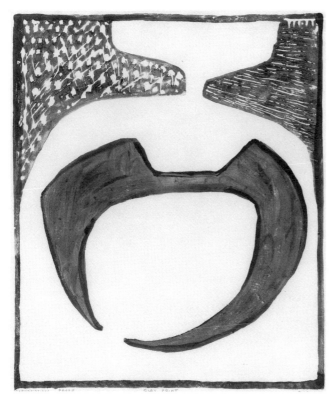

*Annunciation*, 1965, clay print.
Cat. no. 52

In 1966 Marion received her second Canada Council grant for study and travel in Canada and the United States. Her paintings and prints sold fairly regularly, although not for large amounts. An oil painting generally sold for between $300 and $500, while a print would normally sell for $25 to $30. Marion also made nominal sums from monthly rentals of works.[44]

By the end of the 1960s, abstraction was the norm among artists in Calgary and in Alberta in general. Many of the students Marion taught — John Hall, Katie Ohe, Alex Janvier, George Wood — began to make their own marks on the art scene. Nicoll was not forgotten by these artists, but to a certain extent, she slipped from public view, only to be brought to public attention in the late 1970s, after she had ceased to paint.

In 1975, artists John Hall and Ron Moppett put together a retrospective of her work for the Edmonton Art Gallery. The resulting exhibition was shown in Edmonton and in Calgary at the Glenbow Museum. It was around this time that art dealer Peter Ohler first made Marion's acquaintance through her long-standing friend Janet Mitchell. Ohler had heard of Nicoll before meeting her but was not well acquainted with her work. He remembered that when he and Janet Mitchell visited the Nicolls' Bowness home the first time, it was full of Jim Nicoll's work rather than Marion's. Some of her prints and watercolours were stuffed in drawers, but most of her paintings had been relegated to an old shed because Marion had resigned herself to never selling any more of it. Ohler and Mitchell went out to the shed to see what Marion had. They found a bonanza of work stored amid the dust and cobwebs. Seeing what Marion had, Ohler recognized the importance of the work and immediately decided to buy her paintings, prints, watercolours and sketchbooks.[45]

Ohler became committed to bringing Marion's work to public notice, and in 1978 he held a major exhibition of her work at Masters Gallery. In addition to the show, Ohler commissioned a limited edition book on Nicoll by J. Brooks Joyner, *Marion Nicoll - R.C.A.* The exhibition was a success and much of her work sold immediately. Ohler recalled that there was a huge line-up to get into the gallery. Marion was visibly surprised by the acceptance and enthusiasm of the people who attended the exhibition and who subsequently began seeking out her work.

Ohler attributes part of this renaissance in interest and acceptance to economic prosperity of Calgary at the time. The 1970s were a period of expansion, and there was an influx of people from all over the continent. Many of these people had an appreciation of abstract art, and money to spend on it. In any event, the money made from the exhibition and sale of Marion's works was turned over to the artist; it was the most she ever made at one time from the sale of her work.

*Alberta IV, Winter Morning*, 1961, oil on canvas.
Cat. no. 16

*Prairie Railway Siding*, 1967, oil on canvas.
Cat. no. 26

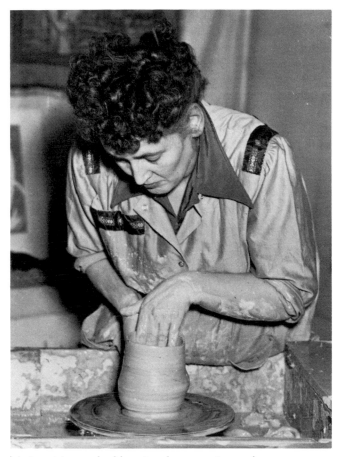

Marion giving a wheelthrowing demonstration at the Alberta Craft Show, Jubilee Auditorium.

## To Guide, Not Lead

One of Marion's major contributions to art in Alberta and Calgary specifically was made through her teaching. Three generations of artists studied with her between 1931, when she started as a student instructor at Tech (which later became the Alberta College of Art), and 1965 when she retired. The list of students, most of whom claim Marion as an important influence in their careers, is impressive: Katie Ohe, George Wood, Stan Perrot, Eileen Taylor, Walt Drohan, Alex Janvier, ManWoman, Bill Panko.

While most of Marion's teaching was done at what was Tech, she also taught at the Banff Summer School, an outgrowth of Leighton's summer courses at Seebe, at the Baker Sanitorium just outside Calgary and extension courses at Black Diamond and Medicine Hat for the University of Alberta.

Marion only taught crafts and design while she was at Tech. She maintained that she avoided teaching painting because she felt that talking about the subject, intellectualizing, got in the way of her own painting.[46] She always claimed that she was not interested in theory, but rather in doing. However, she did manage to pass along her ideas on art through her design course, which every first year student at Tech was required to take. John Hall, who studied with Marion just after her return from New York, remembers that she was full of enthusiasm for abstract painting and would discuss the work of contemporary artists. Eileen Taylor, who studied crafts under Marion, said Marion clearly felt that painting was the highest calling to which one could aspire.[47]

That is not to say that Marion forced her views on her students. She had very clear ideas of what she could and could not do as a teacher. When asked by Duck Ventures (John Hall and Ron Moppett) in an interview for the Edmonton Art Gallery's retrospective of her work in 1975, Marion explained her view that art schools do not turn out artists but:

"only people who are trained to be artists...[one can teach] the craft...how to stretch a canvas, for instance, and prime it and look after your brushes. Do you know something about colour? History of Art? Composition? Design? These are all tools. A little philosophy in understanding yourself, but no push to express yourself. I think you have to learn to draw before you start expressing yourself. I think you have to know the form of the thing sitting in the air and be able to draw it, then what you do with it is your own business."[48]

Marion clearly felt that the artist or craftsman had to come up with his own mode of expression. To try and teach a certain style or direction decapitated the individual's creative process. What she did insist upon was that her students become aware of the implicit rules of painting, ceramics, batik or whatever medium in which they should finally choose to work.

"...whether people like it or not there are rules. And people who go out to break the rules only prove there are rules, otherwise there would be nothing to break...It is natural for the young to rebel against the rules of society...It is almost obligatory for the young artist to do so...the public expects it of him. But there are natural laws that can't be broken. Man, by nature, needs the enclosure of discipline, imposed by society, or built by himself. A man is shaped by the reference of himself to his enclosure. The young throw off society's laws but sometimes neglect to form their own philosophy or viewpoint..."[49]

Marion drew this philosophy of teaching from Leighton. Her students remember that above all she insisted that they work, work, and then do some more work. She maintained that many talented people fail because they do not work but try to slide by. Marion suffered no loafers or prima donnas.

As an instructor, she was keenly aware that she would have an effect on her students and once wrote:

"Instructors can and do cause more harm than good no matter at what level they teach . . . As good potential atheletes can be permanently ruined by poor instruction so can good potential craftsmen be ruined or actors or musicians. Better no instruction at all (people have good instincts if they will use them) than poor instruction."[50]

Stan Perrot points out that she was very serious about her teaching. True to her belief in sound instruction, Marion had to study design, jewellery making, leather craft, weaving, ceramics and batik in order to understand the various media completely herself, so that she could teach a craft to others. It was for this reason that she had gone to the London County Council School of Arts and Crafts to study design in 1937, and to Vancouver to study jewellery making in 1956. Furthermore, there were often few funds available for equipment at Tech, especially in the early days, and according to Perrot, Marion often had to design the equipment to be used in her classes.[51] While students may not have always appreciated the difficulties she faced, they certainly were aware of her wealth of knowledge, her ability to explain her subject, and her support.

One teaching talent Marion clearly had was the ability to let students go their own way to solve a problem in an assignment. She never expected a specific outcome or look to a project. Students were armed with knowledge of materials and how to use them technically but not creatively. Each student was expected only to come up with his or her own solution. The fact that Marion did not teach a certain style or approach as a paradigm may be in part the reason that there is no "Nicollesque" school of artists and craftsmen. Each has developed his or her own style and expression — Marion hated bandwagons, and she could appreciate diverse forms of expression, even if she did not fully understand the message behind them.[52]

A clear example of knowing when not to interfere is highlighted by Marion's approach to Bill Panko. Marion encountered him in 1947 while she was teaching art as a therapy for patients at the Baker Sanitorium, where Panko, a former miner, had been hospitalized with tuberculosis. When he indicated that he was interested in learning how to paint,

Marion taught him the rudiments of watercolour technique. He began to produce strange, naive images drawn from his past experience, images that were sometimes like dreams on paper. Nicoll was taken aback at the images that seemed to pour out of Panko's imagination, and she resisted all attempts by others to influence him. His forms and expressions were his own and no one else's. Partially through Marion's intervention, Panko was given an exhibition at the Coste House in Calgary. His work caused an immediate stir among artists in the city, and paintings were purchased by such leading artists as Max Bates, Janet Mitchell, Cliff Robinson and George Swinton. Later his work was acquired by the National Gallery of Canada. Within five years tuberculosis claimed his life, but Marion had given him an opportunity to express himself and helped him, not directed him, as the need arose.[53]

But it was not only in the classroom that Marion helped her students. There seemed to be no battle too big for Marion. At one point the Department of Indian Affairs felt her wrath when it tried to force artist Alex Janvier to take commercial art rather than fine art at the college. The department threatened to withdraw its financial support if Janvier did not do as he was told. Janvier and Nicoll fought the department to a standstill and it finally relented, allowing Janvier to study painting.[54]

Many of Marion's former students, now teachers themselves, note that her teaching method is duplicated by them in their classrooms and with their students. That insistence on discipline and the basics, providing the technical tools and trying not to impose one's own artistic will upon students, is being passed on to still further generations.

# From Another Perspective

Marion's early works as a child and throughout high school had been grounded in her everyday environment. Drawings of barns, landscape, and friends occupied her through these years. Much of her spare time was taken up with sketching trips to the mountains and surrounding countryside with friends and members of the Calgary Sketch Club and, later, the Alberta Society of Artists.

She also showed an interest in painting still lifes, and a number of these, such as *Pansies* (Cat. no. 30) and *Horse and Vase*, 1943, (Cat. no. 32) survive. Clearly, in these still lifes there is a nascent interest in form and form relationships. They are painted in watercolour, and some bear certain reminiscences of Cezanne, although the forms and perspective are not usually modified in a truly Cezanniste way. Yet these works do display a concern with the interrelationship between curved, circular forms, such as plates, placed in proximity with straight angular forms such as a book in three-quarter view. It was, in fact, a still life which was Marion's first picture to be sold.

In its use of colour, Marion's early landscape work shows the influence of Leighton. She worked from careful sketches, sometimes with colour notation entered into a specific area or at the bottom of a sketch. Marion often tended to a more structural approach than Leighton, making her sketches slightly less open and airy than her teacher's better known works. Into the 1940s one can see a concern with balanced composition and directive elements. Her compositions and point of view are carefully and pleasantly worked out. *Chinook*, 1945 (Cat. no. 1), is an example of one of her better paintings during this time.[55] The arch of the clouds in the upper portion of the painting leads the eye to the right of the composition and is echoed in the curve of the hills, but then the eye is brought back to the centre of the work by the curve of the snowfence which dominates the right lower portion of the painting. The verticality of the individual slats of the fence continually returns the eye to the upper curve, which is then carried over by a sympathetic curve in the furrows of the middle ground in front of the hills. A continual gentle rocking motion is set up. Even one of the horse's necks arches to direct the viewer to the other two horses in the painting. This subtle rolling motion sets up a calm, relaxed feeling that is almost Arcadian in tone. One can almost imagine that these are mythological unicorns rather than horses.

*Pansies*, 1934, watercolour.
Cat. no. 30

A certain serenity or, perhaps more properly, stillness pervades Marion's works throughout this period. *Neilson's Barn*, 1948 (Cat. no. 3), for example, with its off-centre barn occupying a significant portion of the composition, balanced by foreground elements which cut off a corner of the scene and force the eye back into the composition and emphasized by a relatively shallow depth, gives a slightly melancholy air. The colour again is muted and close in tonal value and serves to evoke a feeling of *ennui* brought on by the fact that there are no people, no animals, only quiet stillness.

By the late 1940s, after Nicoll began to privately investigate the subconscious through automatic drawing, a more ominous tone develops in her work.[56] In paintings such as *Badlands at Eladesor* and *Graveyard and Hoodoos* melancholia takes a darker turn. In the second work the whole scene reflects a sober and sombre mind. The white monuments of the graveyards are echoed by the towering hoodoos in the background and ultimately by the mountain in the background. In a manner of speaking, the whole scene becomes a graveyard with the hoodoos as markers of some larger, more cosmic demise than the simple human gravestones, perhaps a planet recently wrenched by war and the newly born nuclear age. The dark tones of the landscape and the tormented sky serve only to make the gravestones more stark, and the inclusion of a funereal black in areas of the accenting weighs heavily. The inclusion of expressively painted, vulturish birds sweeping over a bleak landscape in *Badlands* and sitting on a leafless

*Journey to the Mountains and Return*, 1968-1969, oil on canvas. Collection of the Nickle Arts Museum, University
of Calgary (not included in the exhibition).

*Runes "B"*, 1972, cardboard print.
Cat. no. 60

*Sundogs*, 1967, oil on canvas.
Cat. no. 24

tree in *Graveyard*, hints at something sinister lurking. Its undertones are recalled in an untitled automatic watercolour usually known as *Women, Birds and Reptiles*, 1948 (Cat. no. 34), in which fantastic creatures, odd Druidic caped figures and strange birds abound. There is something clearly unsettling, subconscious and irrational about the image. Its reference is not to perceptual reality but to a murky dream world and the symbolism of the surreal.

After eleven years of dealing with automatic painting and drawing, Marion was ready for the next phase of her development, which began at Emma Lake. The easy, fluid style of the automatics was transferred from the subconscious to the conscious, and Marion's work became more and more abstract. For a brief period, beginning at Emma Lake and continuing forward to her years in New York under Barnet's tutelage, Marion began to take more interest in the figure. In her early work under Barnet's direction, the figure is still discernible. The figure became a central image placed against a background of quadrilateral forms. Such works as *Model* (Cat. no. 44), a watercolour painted in 1958, clearly show how Marion handled the figure at this point. Increasingly, however, Marion began to integrate the figure with the background. As the figure itself becomes more geometric, viewer recognition wanes, until in paintings like *Model and Reflection* (Cat. no. 10) the figure as a discrete form disappeared.

In part, this development of a more personal abstraction can be seen in two of Marion's Sicilian works, *Sicilia III, Fishing Boats* (Cat. no. 7) and *Sicily II, Ulysses Beach* (Cat. no. 6).[57] *Sicilia III* still maintains a clear reference to objective observation. The boat-like forms which are placed throughout the painting in different sizes and colours, culminate in the large form in the lower part of the painting, decorated with the protective eye from the boat's prow or looked at alternately as the head of a fish. We can easily understand that this is a painting of a fleet of fishing boats at anchor in a bay. However, *Sicily II*, is not so easily understood. Although ostensibly a painting of the beach and harbour, we cannot make out the "scene" except for the most rudimentary of associations, such as the association of blue with water or sky. If one looks at Marion's various sketches for the piece, one can begin to see that she has chosen her own points of reference and her own associations of form. The village, the piers and dock disappear as recognizable objects. The objects, the scene, increasingly become starting points from which to paint rather than goals to strive towards recreating.

*Chinook*, 1945, tempera on board.
Cat. no. 1

When Marion returned to Calgary after her experiences in New York and Europe, her work met continued resistance in some quarters. Her bitterness at that lack of acceptance crops up in such paintings as *The Ugly City*, 1964, and *Hostile Place*, 1965. However, her negative feelings were short-lived and by the middle 1960s her work demonstrates an insistent concern with composition, structure, shape and colour, as well as metaphor and symbol.[58]

She expressed her concept of painting when she said: "Painting for me is all on the picture plane, the actual surface of the canvas, with the power held in the horizontal and vertical movements of the expanding colour shapes. There can be, for me, no overlapping, transparencies or fuzzy edges — all these are a hangover from romantic, naturalistic painting."[59]

Marion reached this development by careful consideration and continual re-assessment. She spoke of "battling through the underbrush" to the final image, but her work is never akin to what Albert Elsen calls the warfare between the artist and his canvas which is exhibited in abstract expressionist work such as Wilhelm de Kooning's.[60] Marion's mode of working and her affection for structure, colour and shape preclude the gestural abandon of some strains of abstract expressionism. There was no struggle between the artist and the medium; there is no record of experiment in paint.[61] The battle and the struggle for Marion was fought in her sketchbooks and not with the medium but with the structure of her subject. Her sketchbooks show her passage from perceptual to conceptual structure. Sketches were re-worked, pared down sometimes dozens of times to reach that underlying structure of a subject to reveal those elements that were essential to her. A great part of Marion's abstraction derived from her move from specific to general. In looking at a scene, Marion gave every element within it equal weight and then began to simplify. The first thing to disappear was generally illusionistic space. In effect, Marion flattened the entire scene to come up with two dimensional forms — shapes. Then she began to investigate the parts, balancing their importance with the overall composition. She took parts — perhaps a breast or the arm of a figure, the shape of the space between two elements, say a chair and a table — and re-assembled them in a new context.

Marion sometimes took what might be thought of as opposing shapes, a circular element and a more angular one for example, and juxtaposed them, creating a visual tension in the work.

Marion often gave the immaterial as much weight as the material, for instance, combining the outline of an element with the outline of the ultimate shape, a shadow. On other occasions, she manipulated the scale of certain shapes. Something physically large in a scene might be reduced in the painting, something small inflated. In final painting some elements may be recognizable, but more often they are not. They are usually unrecognizable because they are taken out of their original spatial and material context. The viewer is left with a flat interlocking pattern of forms.[62]

Another source of her abstraction can be traced to her method of using contour drawing. Perhaps influenced by automatic drawing, she used this method not so much to emphasize the edge of an object, but rather the point at which one area bounds another. As Marion would often say, quoting Will Barnet, it was "drawing on both sides of the line." The contour drawing technique abandons modelling in space, and only certain rudimentary admissions of form which affect the overall outline are considered.

Once Marion had arrived at the shapes she wished to use, she began to transfer them to the canvas. Even here changes would be made from the sketches, most often because the necessities of composition in larger scale demanded them. Once the shapes and overall composition were established, she turned

*Neilson's Barn*, 1948-1952, oil on board.
Cat. no. 3

to colour, using it to unify the composition further by the repetition of certain colours, which established the surface, and the inclusion of other colours to accentuate form. Colour can also be used to create spatial effects. Light colours seem nearer to the painted surface than dark colours. Marion counterbalanced the scale of a shape by painting small forms in lighter tones than large elements, as she has in *Bowness Road – 2 a.m.*, 1963 (Cat. no. 19). By doing so, she counteracted the observer's tendency to imagine small forms as farther away from him than larger forms. Marion did not use strict geometric shapes — that is, perfect squares or triangles — but irregular, interlocking shapes which relate to adjacent forms. This also helped her confound the perception of depth. A large dark form would be prevented from becoming part of the background by its fastening to a lighter coloured or neutral tone which would force the eye to read the shapes as being close to the surface of the canvas. Marion's use of interlocking forms rather than truly overlapping shapes further inhibits depth in her work. Just as in a jigsaw, when elements interlock, they do so because they exist on the same plane.

In large measure, this balancing and counterbalancing of the final work was intuitive rather than coldly premeditated. Nicoll herself would recognize what she had done only after the work was finished. While working on a painting, she would have only been aware that certain things did not satisfy her and had to be re-arranged or changed.

*Badlands, Eladesor,* 1953, watercolour.
Cat. no. 40

She said:

"When I'm painting, I paint directly...But when it's done, then I bring my whole critical faculty to bear as to whether it's acceptable or not...You're constantly accepting, rejecting, accepting, rejecting as you paint without even thinking about it, but, afterwards, then, you bring your really critical and decide... You use the whole person, but not necessarily all at one time . . ."[63]

Marion used the nuts and bolts of painting in service of her vision and subject. For example, she normally dispensed with creating texture on her painted surfaces unless it had some direct connection with her subject. While virtually a whole school of tactile abstract art was enjoying favour among abstract expressionists, Marion generally remained true to her shapes

as colours. There are a few instances in which texture does play some part in her work. In *Journey to the Mountains and Return,* 1968-1969, her large triptych, Marion does fill some of her shapes with blobs of colour. In *Guaycura IV, Our Lady of La Paz,* 1966 (Cat. no. 23), there is a meandering line and marking within some of the shapes which heightens the viewer's tendency to read the shapes as being close to the surface plane. Marion also used thick white paint throughout *Our Lady* to suggest the church's white-washed adobe exterior. While these techniques are occasionally used, Marion has done so not to draw attention to her technique but in service of her theme.

Increasingly, Marion began to infuse certain forms and combinations of form with symbolic meaning. Often these symbols were intelligible only to the artist. Some, such as the often present disc symbolizing the sun-moon or season, or the primitive geometric forms such as those in *Ritual II* or *East from the Mountains*, may be discernible to the observer. Others are clearly not. Focusing on the symbols to a certain extent misses the point of Marion's attempt at metaphor. That the viewer's interpretation did not match hers was irrelevant to her. It was not that one could "read" something in a painting, but that one could intuit something from her works that concerned Marion. The only help she offered was a title, which would hint at the source of the image. She was seeking to arouse a common human, subconsciously rooted response to her work. Those archetypal symbols and responses were her goals.

Jim Nicoll maintained that:

"by the time it goes through the metamorphosis of her aesthetic sense, it's, to the general public, unrecognizable, and they have to be satisfied either by explanation or tied in by the title . . . as a matter of fact, there is that unbridgeable gap between the work . . . and the generally cultivated populace."[64]

Marion's paintings have often been criticized as being static. On first consideration one certainly gets an impression of construction, a determined assembly of elements. She used a compositional scheme which she felt was derived from classical sources in which scale, position, balancing of horizontal and vertical elements was carefully worked out and used to organize forms. The canvas was divided and subdivided and elements placed with great care. She abandoned dramatic diagonals which she often used in her early works to push the eye deep into painted space. Marion ceased to concern herself with illusionistic space. Her painting became insistently two-dimensional. Her compositional method gives her work weightiness and a sense of the monumental.

It was Marion's hope to erase the specific and replace it with an underlying universal concept. In this sense the attributes of motion and movement of specific elements would be superficial. When Marion wished to indicate a change or movement, she often did so in subtle ways. In *Maybe, Tomorrow*, 1965 (Cat. no. 51), she broke the circle shape into two parts and increased the scale of one half in relation to the other. She then created a positive-negative effect by changing the colour. It is the movement of the eye from small to corresponding larger form and from light element to dark that is a metaphor for time movement in general. In fact, it is the viewer's awareness, albeit often subconscious, that time is passing as the eye moves from one form to another, that creates time in Marion's work. In a painting such as *Madrid II, Night and Day*, 1960, she created a tunnel-like intrusion into a neighbouring form through which the sun disc could, by extension, move. In this case, it is the awareness that the sun element and the track or tunnel in the

*Graveyard and Hoodoos*, 1955, oil on canvas board. Cat. no. 4

next form are related and that the sun could move along the track that creates time or indicates its transition. What Marion has managed to do is to involve the viewer, and force him to participate in the concept by his investment of the time it takes to look at the painting.[65]

When Marion wished to clearly indicate movement, as in *Migration*, she could easily do so. The sense of movement, of flight, and of repeated seasonal ritual, is made manifest. Marion achieved a suggestion of motion by repeating the basic forms in the painting. She placed the forms against a flat neutral background which does not compete with them for the viewer's attention. The strong horizontal bias of the major elements continually forces the viewer's eye to the left of the canvas. The viewer looks at the repeated horizontal elements and is drawn along the form again and again. The only "brake" Marion put on this movement was the inclusion of three independent vertical lines to the left of the main forms which keep the eye from sweeping off the canvas altogether. Another way in which Marion enhanced movement in the painting was by "weighting" it to the left side, where the horizontal elements are tied together and the elements are most concentrated. There is a natural tendency to move to the most concentrated area, back to the outlying areas of form, and then to be drawn back to the left. This visual "gravity", which promotes eye movement, can be seen as an analogy to the repeated cycles of migration.

Marion saw colour as an integral part of her forms, but she also used it for its subliminal psychological power as well as its compositionally unifying qualities. She virtually never used colour for bald-faced impact.[66] She rarely used pure primary colours. Even in a work as vibrant as *Spring*, 1959, with its reds, blues and yellows, Marion has moderated the potential explosions of colours by working with less intense shades and by placing powerful colours against neutral, flat colour areas which mitigate their intensity. Her colours are not usually "pretty", but she handled them with such ease that they often leave an impression of being livelier in memory than they actually are. Although she moved through different stages in which she used rich, powerful colours, as in *Prophet*, 1960 (Cat. no. 12), or *Alberta IV – Winter Morning*, 1961 (Cat. no. 16), ultimately she tailored her use of colour to specific feelings or environmental conditions rather than pursuing colour for its own sake.

In *Prairie Railway Siding*, 1967 (Cat. no. 26), a later work, Marion used thin washes of colour, painted with short brushstrokes in a way that echoes the undulation of grass or wheat in a field. These "fields" are enclosed by more heavily painted lines to demarcate the form; however, she did not choose to use mimetic colours in these areas. Instead, she selected colours that fitted together harmoniously and fitted an overall scheme that was dictated not by the subject itself, but by her concept of the subject in terms of painting.

Marion's work demonstrates very clearly the modernist notion of a painting as a distinct object which exists in its own right and conforms to the necessities of painting rather than the strictures of perceptual reality. She was one of the first painters in Alberta to take up the modernist cause and move away from art as a "re-creation" of the physical world. She was also one of the first artists in the province to consider painting a function not of what the eye sees, but of how the artist interprets and conceives of what he sees when translating the natural world into paint. What results in Marion's work after 1958 is a promulgation of symbolic and metaphorical forms, sometimes

*Untitled*, no date, pencil on paper.
Cat. no. 77

deeply personal and sometimes immediately accessible, which speaks of her commitment to abstract art and to the environment in which she found herself. In all of her later work, she sought to penetrate the essence of her subject, rather than to define illusionary and transitory appearance. Viewers are required to participate in her work, to think. Marion succeeded in presenting intuitive responses to the universal nature of her environment as exhibited in its specifics. These works succeed as attempts to see the forest without the distraction of the trees.

*Maybe Tomorrow*, 1965, woodcut.
Cat. no. 51

# Notes

1. Laurel Chrumka, taped interview with Marion Nicoll, February, 1982, Glenbow Archives.

2. *Marion Nicoll: A Retrospective 1959 - 1971*, exhibition catalogue, Edmonton Art Gallery, 1975, unpaginated. This and several other quotes are also reproduced, not footnoted, in J. Brooks Joyner's *Marion Nicoll, R.C.A.*, a limited edition book published by Masters Gallery, Calgary, in 1978 in connection with a major exhibition and sale of Marion's work.

3. *Marion Nicoll: A Retrospective.*

4. Ibid, see also Joyner, page 53.

5. Ibid, see also Joyner, page 57.

6. Barbara Leighton, wife of the late A.C. Leighton in taped conversation with the author, August 19, 1985.

7. Chrumka interview with Marion Nicoll.

8. James McLaren Nicoll was born in Fort Macleod, Alberta. He was seventeen years older than Marion. Although he was also an artist, and was present during all the crucial periods of Marion's artistic development - Emma Lake, New York and Europe - there is very little similarity between their work. Except for a brief period of experimentation with abstraction, Jim remained essentially a naturalistic painter. His interest in philosophy and writing may have had some influence on Marion, but it is difficult to determine to what extent. While her association with Jim may have predisposed her towards some theories, it would appear that her most direct influences came through her teachers. Jim Nicoll died January 2, 1986, less than a year after Marion's death.

9. Ibid.

10. *Jock Macdonald: The Inner Landscape*, Joyce Zemans, a catalogue for a retrospective exhibition at The Art Gallery of Ontario, Toronto, 1981, pp. 109-113.

11. *Marion Nicoll: A Retrospective.*

12. Ibid.

13. *Marion Nicoll: A Retrospective.* See also Joyner, page 65. Marion repeatedly claimed that her automatics were strictly an exercise, and in her early experimentation with the technique she did not consider exhibiting them. However, in a letter to Jock Macdonald in the fall of 1948, she must have asked him if she should exhibit them, because in his responding letter to Marion, October 21, 1948, he urged her to submit them for exhibition if she felt they were advanced enough, and in fact, c.1950, Marion did exhibit a piece entitled *Automatic #1.* The original letter from Macdonald to Marion is held in a collection of Macdonald's papers at the McCord Museum, McGill University, Montreal.

14. Of course, Marion was not alone in adapting Jung's theories to art. Ever since the birth of Surrealism in the early part of this century artists have been fascinated with the potential of the unconscious. In addition to psychological interest, such movement as Theosophy, a quasi-religious movement based on a mixture of Eastern religious and Western philosophical thought, gained currency among artists such as Wassily Kandinsky, and Canadians Jock Macdonald and Lawren Harris. These artists strove for the depiction of spiritual essences in their work. Macdonald was also an advocate of the writing of the French artist Ozenfant, whose *Foundation of Modern Art* dealt with similar concepts to Macdonald's modalities and Jung's archetypal forms.

15. Several works mentioned in this catalogue are not in the exhibition. Those works are: *Rain* and *Flight* by Jock Macdonald; and *Journey to the Mountains and Return, Ugly City, Hostile Place, Spring* (1963), and *East River* by Marion Nicoll.

16. Kerr, who had known Macdonald in Vancouver before he came to Calgary, and Blodgett, who was on the Tech staff, both experimented with automatics themselves, although each abandoned the technique. According to Perrot, most of the instructors at Tech during Macdonald's tenure were aware of his experimentation, but were leery of the technique. Kerr in taped conversation with the author, September 17, 1985. Blodgett in a taped conversation with the author, September 5, 1985. Perrot in a taped conversation with the author, August 15, 1985.

17. *Marion Nicoll: A Retrospective.* See also Joyner, page 85.

18. Blodgett related an incident in which a student wishing to discuss Hoffman's theories with Barnet was told to take classes with Hoffman if he wanted to learn his approach.

19. Joyner, page 89.

20. The artistic climate in Calgary was very conservative, and the arts community was divided between established naturalistic painters, who were extremely popular with the public, and a much smaller group of modern painters. Early modernists such as Maxwell Bates and W.L. Stevenson were banned from exhibiting with the Calgary Sketch Club because their work was felt to be too modern.

21. Blodgett interview.

22. As quoted in Joyner, page 87.

23. *October*, *Bow River* and *Untitled* (Cat. no. 41) in this exhibition were originally purchased at that sale.

24. *Marion Nicoll: A Retrospective*. See also Joyner, page 93.

25. Marion made this comment in a letter to Jean Johnston, Calgary, November 19, 1958. A photocopy of this letter is in the Marion Nicoll files in the Glenbow Archives.

26. Marion Nicoll in a letter to Jean Johnston, Calgary, October 9, 1958. A photocopy of this letter is in the Marion Nicoll files in the Glenbow Archives.

27. Marion Nicoll in a letter to Jean Johnston, Calgary, November 19, 1958. A photocopy of this letter is in the Marion Nicoll files in the Glenbow Archives.

28. *Marion Nicoll: A Retrospective*. See also Joyner, page 97.

29. Marion Nicoll in a letter to Jean Johnston, Calgary, February 25, 1959. A photocopy of this letter is in the Marion Nicoll files in the Glenbow Archives.

30. Ibid.

31. Marion Nicoll in a letter to Jean Johnston, Calgary, June 10, 1959. A photocopy of this letter is in the Marion Nicoll files in the Glenbow Archives.

32. Terry Fenton suggests that Marion was influenced by Adolph Gottlieb in this painting because the forms are compartmentalized. Marion may have been aware of Gottlieb's pictographs at the time, but it seems to the author that the subject may have imposed the imagery and Gottlieb is a secondary influence in this case. See "Some artists in Regina and Saskatoon", Terry Fenton, *Arts Canada*, February/March, 1971.

33. John Hall, a student of Marion's at A.C.A. following her return from New York and Europe noted that she was eager to share her knowledge and approach to abstract art. John Hall in a taped conversation with the author June 6, 1985.

34. See "Clement Greenberg's View of Art on the Prairies", Clement Greenberg, *Canadian Art*, vol. xx, no.2, March/April 1963, page 96.

35. Joyner, page 101.

36. Marion Nicoll account book, in the possession of Janet Mitchell, Calgary. A photocopy of this account book is in the Marion Nicoll files in the Glenbow Archives.

37. Marion had been involved in printmaking before this time and had originally gone to Emma Lake to study printmaking. However, later in her career, when painting became too strenuous because of her arthritis, she concentrated more heavily on the medium. Several of her important exhibitions were print shows.

38. Will Barnet in a letter to Marion and Jim Nicoll, August 20, 1961. This letter is in the Marion Nicoll files in the Glenbow Archives.

39. Greenberg op. cit. Marion met Greenberg through Jock Macdonald when she was in New York, but it is unclear whether or not he ever visited her studio or was familiar with her work there.

40. See "14 Monumental Gestures", Ken Winters, *The Winnipeg Free Press*, January 30, 1965.

41. See "The Debonair Joyce Caught in Bronze", Edward Barry, *Chicago Tribune*, February 25, 1968.

42. See "Four Women and the Circle", Donald Anderson, *Chicago's American*, February 18, 1968.

43. Will Barnet in a letter to Jim and Marion Nicoll July 15, 1962. This letter is in the Marion Nicoll files in the Glenbow Archives.

44. Marion's account book reveals that her income from art rentals and sales for prints and paintings during the 1960s rose from a low of just under $1,310 in 1964 to a high of nearly $3,900 in 1969.

45. Peter Ohler in a taped conversation with the author September 25, 1985.

46. Despite this claim, a number of Marion's students remember her talking about painting and painters during her classes.

47. Hall interview. Eileen Taylor in a taped conversation with the author July 11, 1985.

48. *Marion Nicoll: A Retrospective*.

49. Ibid.

50. Marion Nicoll lecture notes, undated, in the Marion Nicoll files in the Glenbow Archives.

51. Perrot interview.

52. Marion commented that she could appreciate a work of art without having to understand it and she welcomed contemporary developments. Chrumka interview.

53. Chrumka interview.

54. Ibid. Marion's kindnesses to students were legendary. George Wood, who studied with Marion in the 1950s, noted that on many occasions students attending Tech from out of town and unable to go home for Christmas were invited to the Nicolls' for Christmas dinner. Clifford Robinson remembered that when he was student and began to take wood block printing, it was Marion who provided him with his first set of professional tools. Several years later she asked him to return them so she could give them to another student. Artist ManWoman, who also studied with Marion at A.C.A. in the 1960s, said that she once gave him a small grant out of her pocket and asked only that he do the same for a promising student should he encounter one in need. George Wood in a taped interview with the author June 5, 1985. Clifford Robinson in a taped conversation with the author August 14, 1985. ManWoman in a response to a questionnaire from the author August, 1985.

55. During this period Marion did several watercolours which feature a strong element such as a fence or a log in the foreground and in which the eye is drawn back into the painting by a road or river. *Chinook* and *The Bird's Nest*, 1948, are examples of how Marion gradually moved to a more subtle manipulation of depth and eye movement in a painting.

56. If one looks at the watercolours Marion was painting during this period, one notes the use of swirling, almost agitated elements in the handling of water and trees limbs. These elements are almost certainly the result of her experience with automatics.

57. It is believed that *Sicily II, Ulysses Beach* was actually painted in Sicily. Marion had mentioned in a letter to Jean Johnston that she was only going to take small canvases with her because they would be easier to transport. *Sicily I, Sirocco* and *Sicilia III, Fishing Boats* were painted after Marion's return to Canada.

58. *The Ugly City* and *Hostile Place* were part of a reaction on Marion's part to early resistance to her abstract work when she returned from Europe. However, she moved beyond that reaction as she noted in *Marion Nicoll: A Retrospective*. "I've also eliminated some hostilities which I had such as that 'Hostile Place' and the people, the city, the people buried in concrete. . . I got rid of that completely. . . I've gone away from everything but landscape."

59. *Marion Nicoll: A Retrospective.*

60. See Albert E. Elsen, *Purposes of Art*, Holt, Rinehart and Winston, Inc.: New York, 1972, second edition.

61. In addition, Marion's paintings are generally quite small by most contemporary standards. Marion painted almost exclusively on an easel, a method that was virtually abandoned by painters in the 1950s and 1960s. Jackson Pollock, for example, placed his canvas on the floor to allow himself more freedom of movement around the canvas.

Other painters, such as Morris Louis who used a pouring technique to create veils of colour, eschewed the easel as well. Towards the end of the 1950s and again into the 1960s, painters began to make works of such huge scale that using an easel was ruled out.

62. Marion also noted that the grid-like formation of her landscapes sometimes is derived from an aerial point of view. Such a point of view strengthens the flat, pattern-like appearance of a scene. In *Marion Nicoll: A Retrospective* she mentions a work that resulted from an airplane trip.

63. Wood interview. Two works in the exhibition, *Prairie Railway Siding* and *Prairie Farm* are quite severe in their abstraction heightened by an aerial view of the scene. But even these, when compared to the works of the artists mentioned, are not as "hard-edged."

64. Jim Nicoll in a transcript for a video-taped interview with Jim and Marion, January 29, 1973. Helen Wright (audio) and Ingrid Mercer (video).

65. Such potential or imminent movement can be seen in the work of artists in non-literate cultures as well as in the work of ancient narrative painters in European history. It was a way of indicating a change of time within the same painting. Medieval narrative painters depicting a story often repeated the same individuals progressing through a series of episodes. They would use scale and positioning to quite literally demonstrate how close to us in time the events occurred. Early episodes appeared "farther back" in the painting with small scale figures, the climax and last episode appeared close to the surface plane with correspondingly larger figures. Early Renaissance artists would often change the scale of figures in donor portraits. The donors would appear as smaller figures, while the religious figure would be in scale with the rest of the scene in the painting. In this way the spiritual and physical realms within the painting were separated.

66. Marion associated certain colours with certain concepts and moods. For example, she considered blue a sensitive and rational colour, while purple was profound and mystical. One can see a correlation between the colours Marion used in paintings such as *Prophet* and *Our Lady of La Paz* and the subject matter of the painting. Marion presented a lecture to the Calgary Paint, Oil and Varnish Club in March 1950 on the psychology of colour. A copy of her typed outline is in the Marion Nicoll files in the Glenbow Archives.

*Birth of a Legend*, 1971, clay print.
Cat. no. 59

# Bibliography and Research Sources

## Articles

"Marion Nicoll 1909 - 1985," *Visual Arts Newsletter*, (Alberta Culture) Vol. 7, no. 2, issue 28, April, 1985.

"Pioneering local artist dies after long illness," Nancy Tousley, *Calgary Herald*, March 7, 1985.

"Seeing it Our Way," Sat Kumer Producer, Jerry Olson Executive Producer, Marion Nicoll, CBC documentary segment produced July 2, 1982, broadcast September 16, 1982, CBC Calgary Film Library.

"Tribute to Nicolls," Robert Nadeau, *Arts West* 7:3:43, March 1982.

" 'Tribute' Centennial Library Until March 31," Evelyn Blakeman, *Edmonton Journal*, March 25, 1982.

"Tribute to the Nicolls, Marriage of ideas merges between the two artists," Nancy Tousley, *Calgary Herald*, January 27, 1982.

"Living legends make return for tribute exhibition," Patrick Tivy, *Calgary Herald*, Thursday, January 21, 1982.

"Surrealism and Marion Nicoll," Christopher Varley, *Update*, (Edmonton Art Gallery) Vol. 2, No. 5, September/October 1981.

"Work reflects orderly eye," Evelyn Blakeman, *Edmonton Journal*, January 24, 1979.

"Natural imagery dominates work," Brooks Joyner, *The Albertan*, December 3, 1978, visual arts section.

Review "Marion Nicoll," Brooks Joyner, *Arts West* 3:2:32-35, March/April 1978.

"Calgary artists Marion and Jim Nicoll: 'People thought we would be painting forever'," Joy-Ann Cohen, *Calgary Herald*, March 25, 1978.

"Nicoll's clay prints 'mature, interesting'," Jean Richards, *Edmonton Journal*, March 22, 1978.

"A tribute to Nicoll," Brooks Joyner, *The Albertan*, March 3, 1978.

"Nicoll retrospective focuses on abstracts," Carol Hogg, *Calgary Herald*, June, 1975.

"Nicoll: Stunning discovery," Victor Arcega, *The Albertan*, June 7, 1975.

"Nicoll retrospective - development of an artist," Jean Richards, *Edmonton Journal*, June 7, 1975.

"Marion Nicoll retrospective, more than 40 paintings ago," *Calgary Herald*, May 31, 1975.

"Marion Nicoll show to open art gallery," *Edmonton Journal*, March 24, 1975.

"Art gathered from city homes for showing," J.A. Forbes, *Edmonton Journal*, 1973.

"Some artists in Regina and Saskatoon," Terry Fenton, *Arts Canada*, February/March, 1971.

"A child-like approach," Linda Curtis, *The Albertan*, December 6, 1969.

"Artist wins coin contest," *The Albertan*, June 18, 1969.

"The Debonair Joyce Caught in Bronze," Edward Barry, *Chicago Tribune*, February 25, 1968.

"Four Women and the Circle," Donald Anderson, *Chicago's American*, February 18, 1968.

"Abstract art with a cigarillo," *The Albertan*, July 14, 1967.

"Artist Plans Constant Work To 'Earn' $5,500 Scholarship," Mary Biner, *Calgary Herald*, 1966.

"Marion Nicoll Work Praised," David Thompson, *Calgary Herald*, April 18, 1966.

"Paintings by Marion Nicoll," Biographical Notes by Harry Kiyooka, Western Canada Art Circuit, September 21, 1965.

"14 Monumental Gestures," Ken Winters, *The Winnipeg Free Press*, January 30, 1965.

"Life and Painting Synonymous for Calgary Artist-Teacher," Adeline Flaherty, *Calgary Herald*, January 27, 1965.

"Ancient Wax Painting Form Being Taught At Art College," Mary Biner, *Calgary Herald*, January 8, 1965.

"Art Show Features Boldness Of Nicoll's Abstract Works," Robin Neesham, *Calgary Herald*, December 10, 1963.

"Exhibit By Nichol (sic) Last For Gallery," Dorothy Barnhouse, *Edmonton Journal*, October 19, 1963.

"Artists' Own Walk-Up Gallery Closing With Nicoll Exhibit," Dorothy Barnhouse, *Edmonton Journal*, October 19, 1963.

"Clement Greenberg's View of Art on the Prairies," Clement Greenberg, *Canadian Art*, vol. xx, no. 2, March/April 1963.

"Painter Teaches Craft Classes," Jenni Morton, *Calgary Herald*, February 6, 1963.

"Gallery Exhibition Thursday," *Edmonton Journal*, January 26, 1963.

"The Journal of The Arts," Desmond Bill, *Edmonton Journal*, June 23, 1962.

"Variety Defeats Tyranny of Taste," *Toronto Globe and Mail*, October 7, 1961.

"Calgary Boasts Woman Expert in Batik Art," *The Amherstburg Echo*, January 9, 1958.

Untitled article from *The Albertan*, November 30, 1957.

"Teacher Favors Experimental Art; Husband Doesn't Share Opinions," Dushan Bresky, *Calgary Herald*, January 26, 1953.

"Artist Gives Advice On Buying Paintings," *Calgary Herald*, December 7, 1951.

## Books and Catalogues

Robert Doty. *Will Barnet*. New York: Harry N. Abrams, Inc., Publishers, 1984.

*Marion Nicoll, A Retrospective*. Interview by Duck Ventures, (John Hall and Ron Moppett). Exhibition catalogue. Edmonton: Edmonton Art Gallery, 1975.

Albert E. Elsen. *Purposes of Art*. New York: Holt, Rinehart and Winston, Inc., 1972, second edition.

Northrop Frye. *Anatomy of Criticism*. Princeton, New Jersey: Princeton University Press, 1957.

J. Russell Harper. *Painting in Canada: A History*. Toronto: University of Toronto Press, 1966.

J. Brooks Joyner. *Marion Nicoll R.C.A.*. Calgary: Masters Gallery Ltd., 1978.

Colin S. Macdonald. *A Dictionary of Canadian Artists* Vol. 5. Ottawa: Canadian Paperback Publishers Ltd., 1977.

Ladislav Matejka and Irwin Titunik, editors. *Semiotics of Art*. Cambridge, Massachusetts and London, England: The M.I.T. Press, 1976.

Amedee Ozentfant. *Foundations of Modern Art*. New York: Dover Publications Inc., 1952. Revised edition from 1931 edition; John Rodker, publisher.

Dennis Reid. *A Concise History of Canadian Painting*. Toronto: Oxford, 1973.

Harold Rosenberg. *Art on the Edge*. Chicago and London: The University of Chicago Press, 1983 edition.

The University of Victoria. *Creative Canada* Vol. 1. Victoria: The Reference Division of McPherson Library, 1971.

Christopher Varley. *Winnipeg West: Painting and Sculpture in Western Canada, 1945-1970*. Exhibition catalogue. Edmonton: Edmonton Art Gallery, 1983.

Joyce Zemans. *Jock Macdonald: The Inner Landscape, A Retrospective Exhibition*. Exhibition catalogue. Toronto: Art Gallery of Ontario, 1981.

## Research Sources

The Marion Nicoll Papers, Glenbow Museum Archives, Calgary, Alberta.

The Jock Madonald Papers, McCord Museum Library, Montreal, Quebec.

Transcript of interview of Marion and Jim Nicoll with Helen Wright for Glenbow Museum video-tape X20-15, January 29, 1973.

Taped interview with Marion Nicoll February, 1982. Interviewer, Laurel Chrumka for Glenbow Museum.

Taped interview with George Wood, June 5, 1985.

Taped interview with John Hall, June 6, 1985.

Taped interview with Eileen Taylor, July 11, 1985.

Prepared Questionnaire, ManWoman, August, 1985.

Taped interview with Clifford Robinson, August 14, 1985.

Taped interview with Stanford Perrott, August 15, 1985.

Taped interview with Barbara Leighton, August 19, 1985.

Taped interview with Stan Blodgett, September 5, 1985.

Taped interview with Illingworth Kerr, September 17, 1985.

Taped interview with Peter Ohler, September 25, 1985.

## Artists' Files

A.C. Leighton artist file, Art Department, Glenbow Museum.

James McLaren Nicoll artist file, Art Department, Glenbow Museum.

Marion Nicoll artist file, Art Department, Glenbow Museum.

# Chronology

**1909:**
April 11, Marion Florence Mackay was born in Calgary, Alberta. Her father Robert Mackay was a Scottish immigrant from Thurso who came to Calgary in 1886. He eventually became the head of the city's electrical engineering department. Her mother, Florence Gingras, was of French and Irish descent and was born in Michigan. The family immigrated to Canada and eventually settled in Evarts, Alberta.

**1911:**
Sister Isobel born.

**c.1914:**
Entered Central Public School (later known as James Short Public School)

**c.1923:**
Entered Central High School

**c.1924:**
Despite being from a Presbyterian family, transferred to St. Joseph's Convent, Red Deer for one year.

**1925:**
Returned to Central High School. Studied art with R.L. Harvey and with his encouragement decided to go to art school. Did not finish high school.

**1926:**
Entered Ontario College of Art, Toronto. J.E.H. MacDonald was the principal. Arthur Lismer and Franz Johnston were teachers. Marion studied design under Johnston. She studied at O.C.A. for two years.

**1929:**
Younger sister Isobel died of pneumonia. This was the second death from pneumonia in the family. A brother had died before Marion's birth. Marion's mother refused to let Marion return to Toronto because she had returned to Calgary suffering from anemia and weight loss. Marion transferred to the Provincial Institute of Technology and Art (known at the time as Tech). First met A.C. Leighton, head of the school. Leighton put Marion back into first year because he felt she had not learned to draw or use colour in Toronto. Three months later Marion advanced back into third year.

**1931:**
Leighton made Marion a student instructor at Tech. First met James McLaren Nicoll, seventeen years her senior, at a Calgary Sketch Club meeting. Jim Nicoll, born in Fort Macleod, was an engineer and artist.

Marion at 17, before leaving for
the Ontario College of Art, c.1926.

**1932 - 1933:**
Leighton invited Marion to his summer classes at Seebe. This summer session was the beginning of the Banff Summer School in visual arts.

**1933:**
After graduating from Tech, Marion became an instructor in crafts and design at Tech. Leighton left Tech due to ill health and was replaced by British-born H.G. Glyde, who had been an instructor at the school.

**1936:**
Became a member of the Alberta Society of Artists.

**1937:**
Took a year's leave from Tech to go to London, England to study design at London County Council School of Arts and Crafts. Travelled to Britain by ship down the west coast of North America, through the Panama Canal and to Britain. Stopped in San Francisco along the way. While studying in Britain, Marion visited the National Gallery and Tait Museum. She also travelled throughout England and Scotland, as well as making a trip to Norway, Sweden and Denmark. In December, Marion's mother died, but her father urged her to stay in Britain and finish her studies.

**1938:**
Marion returned to Calgary and resumed teaching at Tech.

**1940 - 1942:**
Marion and Jim Nicoll were married in 1940. Marion left Tech. During World War Two Jim Nicoll worked as an engineer for the Royal Canadian Air Force and was transferred around the West to supervise building of air bases. Marion and Jim moved sixteen times during this period. They finally rented a house in Bowness, then a village west of Calgary city limits.

Marion during a bicycle trip in Britain, c.1938.

**1945:**
Marion and Jim moved to a small house in Bowness in which they lived until 1981. Marion began teaching at the Baker Sanitorium near her home. She met Bill Panko, a former miner, who was suffering from tuberculosis of the hip. She taught him the rudiments of watercolour painting and was instrumental in bringing him to the attention of A.F. Key, Director of the Allied Arts Council. Panko was given a solo exhibition at Coste House in Calgary.

**1946:**
Marion returned to teaching at Tech under the new head J.W.G. "Jock" Macdonald. She also taught university extension courses in Medicine Hat and Black Diamond for the University of Alberta. Marion discovered that Macdonald was experimenting with automatic drawing and asked him to demonstrate the technique. Marion began a daily regimen of doing automatics as Macdonald had instructed her. She maintained that regimen for eleven years. These works were not exhibited until the late 1970s. During the summer she taught at the Banff Summer School. Macdonald, Andre Bieler, A.Y. Jackson, and Walter Phillips were among the teaching staff. At this time Marion was working primarily in watercolours and concentrating on crafts.

**1950:**
Marion began suffering from arthritis.

**1956:**
Marion visited Vancouver and learned jewellery making techniques.

**1957:**
Marion and Jim, along with Illingworth Kerr, Stanford Blodgett and Stanford Perrot, attended an Emma Lake Workshop organized by Regina College, University of Saskatchewan. Marion intended to study printmaking under Will Barnet, a teacher from the Art Students' League in New York. The printing supplies did not arrive and Barnet taught watercolour classes instead. Under Barnet's tutelage Marion abandoned her naturalistic style and began to paint abstractions. Following the workshop Marion and Jim decided that they would go to New York the following year to study with Barnet at the Art Students' League.

**1958:**
Marion and Jim held a yard sale of paintings to raise money for their move to New York. Marion sold watercolours for $5 apiece and drawings for $2. Marion took an unpaid leave of absence from Tech and she and Jim left for New York. Both Marion and Jim enrolled at the Art Students' League. Marion studied with Barnet until the spring of 1959.

**1959:**
Marion was offered a teaching position at Cooper Union, a design museum in New York. Will Barnet and painter Barnett Newman urged Marion to stay in New York and continue painting. Because Jim disliked the city and she felt duty-bound to return to teaching in Calgary, Marion decided not to stay. While studying in New York Marion received word that she had been given a Canada Council grant. Marion and Jim used the money to finance a trip to Sicily, Italy, Portugal and Spain. The bulk of their two-month stay was spent in Sicily, however, they also visited Florence, Rome, Ravenna, and Assisi in Italy; Toledo and Madrid in Spain and Lisbon and the Azores in Portugal. On the way home to Calgary, Marion and Jim stopped in Duluth, Minnesota to visit Barnet who was teaching there. Upon returning to Calgary, Marion returned to Tech (now known as the Alberta College of Art).

**1966:**
Marion's arthritis had become so severe that she could no longer teach at A.C.A. She retired in January. Marion received a second Canada Council Fellowship. She used the grant to travel across Canada and to visit Barnet in New York.

**1969:**
She was commissioned to design a wall for a campground near Tilley, Alberta. Designed playground equipment for Environment '69 in collaboration with architect Conrad Loban.

**1970:**
Marion's arthritis was so severe that she virtually ceased to paint. She had her first major operation. Marion received an honourable mention from the Royal Canadian Mint for her design of the reverse side of a coin celebrating Manitoba's centennial.

Marion in studio with students' paintings, c.1955.

**1975**:
New interest developed in Marion's art and her first retrospective was organized by John Hall, a former student, and Ron Moppett.

**1977**:
Marion was elected a member of the Royal Canadian Academy. Peter Ohler, owner of Masters Gallery, was introduced to Marion and Jim by Marion's friend Janet Mitchell. Ohler purchased all of the work Marion had in her possession and mounted a major exhibition of her work at his Calgary gallery. Ohler also commissioned a biography of Nicoll's life by J. Brooks Joyner.

**1981**:
Marion's arthritis became so bad that she had to leave her home in Bowness and enter the Bethany Care Centre. However, Marion took a continuing interest in art. She organized the acquisition of artworks for decoration of the Centre.

**1985**:
Marion died of a heart attack, March 6, 1985.

# Catalogue of the Exhibition

*In all cases height precedes width in measurements. Conversions have been mechanically calculated from Imperial measurements.

Exhibition histories in print section note that one image from the edition was exhibited.

*Images appear above their Catalogue entry.

## Oils, Acrylics, Temperas and Encaustics

1. **Chinook**, 1945,
tempera on board,
37.0 x 50.0 cm,
Collection of the Nickle Arts Museum,
University of Calgary

2. **The Bird's Nest**, 1948,
oil on canvas,
40.6 x 50.8 cm, (by conversion),
Exhibited: Coste House, Calgary, c.1949,
Private Collection

3. **Neilson's Barn**, 1948-1952,
oil on board,
31.4 x 38.1 cm, (image),
Collection of the Alberta Art Foundation

4. **Graveyard and Hoodoos**, 1955,
oil on canvas board,
50.7 x 40.5 cm,
Collection of the Alberta Art Foundation

5. **Sicilia I, Sirocco**, 1959,
oil on canvas,
71.1 x 91.5 cm,
Exhibited: Faculty Exhibition (Tech), 1959;
Bowness Town Hall, 1960; Upstairs Gallery, Toronto, 1961;
Allied Arts Centre, Calgary, 1963; Marion Nicoll: A
Retrospective, Edmonton and Calgary, 1975,
Collection of the Alberta Art Foundation

6. **Sicily II, Ulysses Beach**, 1959,
oil on canvas,
45.7 x 53.2 cm,
Exhibited: Faculty Exhibition (Tech), 1959;
Bowness Town Hall, 1960; Allied Arts Centre,
Calgary, 1963,
Collection of the Glenbow Museum

7. **Sicilia III, Fishing Boats**, 1959,
oil on canvas,
76.2 x 106.7 cm, (by conversion),
Exhibited: Faculty Exhibition (Tech), 1959;
Bowness Town Hall, 1960; Allied Arts Centre,
Calgary, 1963
Private Collection

8. **Spring**, 1959,
oil on canvas,
91.8 x 71.7 cm,
Exhibited: Faculty Exhibition (Tech), 1959;
Alberta Society of Artists exhibition, Calgary, 1961;
New Acquisitions, Glenbow Museum, 1984,
Collection of Glenbow Museum,
purchased with funds from the
Canada Council and Esso Resources Canada Limited

9. **Self Portrait**, 1959,
oil on canvas,
60.9 x 76.2 cm, (by conversion),
Exhibited: Bowness Town Hall, 1960;
Allied Arts Centre, Calgary, 1963;
Marion Nicoll: A Retrospective,
Edmonton and Calgary, 1975,
E.D.D. Tavender Collection

10. **Model and Reflection**, 1960,
oil on canvas,
91.4 x 60.9 cm, (by conversion),
Private Collection

11. **Presence, A Friend**, 1960,
oil on canvas,
102.0 x 112.5 cm,
Exhibited: Upstairs Gallery, Toronto, 1961;
'Focus', Edmonton, 1962,
Permanent Collection, University Collections,
University of Alberta

12. **Prophet**, 1960
oil on canvas,
106.7 x 82.6 cm, (by conversion),
Exhibited: Marion Nicoll, R.C.A.,
Masters Gallery, Calgary, 1978,
Collection of Shirley and Peter Savage

13. **Madrid II, Night and Day**, 1960,
oil on canvas,
61.3 x 106.7 cm,
Exhibited: Bowness Town Hall, 1960;
Upstairs Gallery, Toronto, 1961;
"Focus", Edmonton, 1962,
Collection of the Art Gallery of Hamilton,
gift of Glen E. Cumming, 1982

14. **East from the Mountains**, 1961,
oil on canvas,
102.2 x 137.2 cm, (by conversion),
Exhibited: Marion Nicoll: A Retrospective,
Edmonton and Calgary, 1975,
Collection of the University of Lethbridge,
gift of Gordon and Elizabeth Gibbs, Calgary, 1982

15. **Prairie Winter II, Moon in the Morning**, 1961,
oil on canvas,
96.5 x 154.9 cm, (by conversion),
Also known as **Prairie Alberta II,
Moon in the Morning**,
Exhibited: Marion Nicoll: A Retrospective,
Edmonton and Calgary, 1975,
Collection of Gerald N. Pencer

16. **Alberta IV, Winter Morning**, 1961
oil on canvas,
99.0 x 116.8 cm, (by conversion),
Exhibited: Allied Arts Centre, Calgary,
1963; Marion Nicoll: A Retrospective,
Edmonton and Calgary, 1975
Private Collection

17. **Ancient Wall**, 1962,
oil on canvas,
107.6 x 153.2 cm,
Exhibited: Marion Nicoll: A Retrospective,
Edmonton and Calgary, 1975; Winnipeg West,
travelling exhibition, organized by
Edmonton Art Gallery, 1983,
The Edmonton Art Gallery Collection,
gift of Beta Sigma Phi, 1963

18. **City Lights**, 1962,
oil on canvas,
53.3 x 152.4 cm, (by conversion),
Private Collection

19. **Bowness Road, 2 a.m.**, 1963,
oil on canvas,
136.0 x 186.0 cm,
Exhibited: Allied Arts Centre, Calgary, 1963;
Contemporary Art from the Permanent Collection,
Glenbow Museum, 1985; Marion Nicoll Memorial
Display, Glenbow Museum, 1985,
Collection of Glenbow Museum

20. **Ritual II**, 1963,
oil on canvas,
128 x 152.8 cm,
Also known as **Birth Ritual**,
Exhibited: Allied Arts Centre, Calgary, 1963,
Collection of Alberta Art Foundation

21. **Eclipse**, 1963,
oil on canvas,
127.0 x 101.6 cm, (by conversion),
Exhibited: Marion Nicoll: A Retrospective,
Edmonton and Calgary, 1975,
Collection of Mrs. Betty Anne Graves

22. **Migration**, 1964,
oil on canvas,
115.5 x 143.7 cm, (framed),
Collection of Nickle Arts Museum,
University of Calgary

23. *Guaycura IV, Our Lady of La Paz*, 1966,
oil on canvas,
114.3 x 137.2 cm, (by conversion),
Exhibited: Alberta Society of Artists exhibition, 1967;
Marion Nicoll: A Retrospective,
Edmonton and Calgary, 1975,
Collection of Joan and Dale Simmons

24. *Sundogs*, 1967,
oil on canvas,
137.2 x 114.3 cm,
Collection of the London Regional Art Gallery

25. *Untitled*, 1967,
acrylic on canvas,
114.8 x 101.8 cm,
Collection of the Alberta Art Foundation

26. *Prairie Railway Siding*, 1967,
oil on canvas,
92.0 x 107.0 cm,
Collection of the Alberta Art Foundation

27. *January '68*, 1969,
oil on canvas,
137.2 x 114.3 cm,
Collection of the Alberta Art Foundation

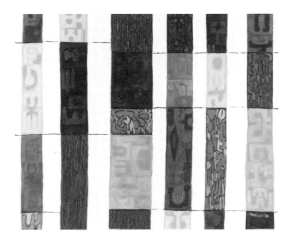

28. *Snow fence at Canmore*, 1970,
oil on canvas,
112.0 x 122.0 cm,
Also known as **Canmore, Deer Fence**,
Collection of Shell Canada Limited

29. *God out of the Night*, 1959,
encaustic on masonite board,
77.0 x 31.2 cm, (image),
Collection of the Leighton Foundation

## Watercolours

30. *Pansies*, 1934,
watercolour,
25.2 x 17.8 cm,
Collection of the Alberta Art Foundation

31. *Brewster's*, 1935,
watercolour and ink,
15.1 x 11.7 cm,
Collection of the Alberta Art Foundation

32. *Horse and Vase*, 1943,
watercolour,
38.1 x 27.9 cm, (by conversion),
Collection of Mr. and Mrs. Pierre Hetu, Edmonton

33. *Untitled*, 1948,
automatic watercolour,
30.0 x 22.5 cm,
The Edmonton Art Gallery Collection,
purchased in 1981 with funds donated by
Gulf Canada Oil Limited

34. **Untitled (Woman, with Reptiles and Birds),** 1948,
automatic watercolour,
27.5 x 20.0 cm,
Exhibited: Winnipeg West, travelling exhibition,
organized by Edmonton Art Gallery, 1983;
Contemporary Art from the Permanent Collection,
Glenbow Museum, 1985; Marion Nicoll Memorial
Display, Glenbow Museum, 1985,
Collection of the Glenbow Museum,
gift of Mr. Peter Ohler,
Masters Gallery Limited, 1980

35. **Untitled**, May 1, 1948,
automatic watercolour,
18.9 x 15.3 cm, (image),
Collection of the Glenbow Museum

36. **Untitled**, August 14, 1948,
automatic watercolour,
30.1 x 22.6 cm,
Collection of the Glenbow Museum,
gift of Mr. Peter Ohler,
Masters Gallery Limited, 1980

37. **Untitled**, November 13, 1948,
automatic watercolour,
30.1 x 22.6 cm,
Exhibited: Marion Nicoll Memorial Display,
Glenbow Museum, 1985,
Collection of the Glenbow Museum,
gift of Mr. Peter Ohler,
Masters Gallery Limited, 1980

38. **Untitled**, November 14, 1948,
automatic watercolour,
30.1 x 22.6 cm,
Collection of the Glenbow Museum,
gift of Mr. Peter Ohler,
Masters Gallery Limited, 1980

39. **Metamorphosis**, 1950,
automatic watercolour,
29.9 x 21.6 cm,
Exhibited: Marion Nicoll, R.C.A.,
Masters Gallery, Calgary, 1978,
Collection of Petro-Canada Limited

40. *Badlands, Eladesor*, 1953,
watercolour,
35.6 x 44.2 cm,
Exhibited: Alberta Society of Artists
travelling exhibition, date uncertain;
Marion Nicoll Memorial Display,
Glenbow Museum, 1985
Collection of the Glenbow Museum
purchased with Alberta 75th Anniversary funds

41. *Untitled*, no date, (before 1958),
watercolour,
38.1 x 27.9 cm, (by conversion),
Collection of M. Moss

42. *Bow River*, no date, (before 1958),
watercolour,
30.5 x 35.7 cm, (by conversion),
Collection of Mrs. Eileen Taylor

43. *October*, 1956,
watercolour,
34.3 x 40.6 cm, (by conversion),
Collection of Mrs. Eileen Taylor

44. *The Model*, 1958,
watercolour,
27.7 x 21.3 cm,
Exhibited: Marion Nicoll, R.C.A.,
Masters Gallery, Calgary, 1978,
Collection of the Alberta Art Foundation

45. *The Model with Green Towel*, 1958,
watercolour,
26.0 x 18.6 cm, (image),
Exhibited: Marion Nicoll, R.C.A.,
Masters Gallery, Calgary, 1978,
Petro-Canada Art Collection

46. *Untitled*, 1972,
automatic watercolour,
22.7 x 30.5 cm,
The Edmonton Art Gallery Collection,
purchased in 1978 with funds donated
by The Downstairs Gallery, Edmonton
and Otis Elevator Company, Limited

## Prints

47. *Expanding White*, 1960,
clay print on J-cloth,
19.1 x 25.4 cm, (image),
Exhibited: Marion Nicoll: A Retrospective,
Edmonton and Calgary, 1975,
Collection of the Alberta Art Foundation

48. *Butterflies*, 1963,
clay print,
28.0 x 34.3 cm,
Collection of the Glenbow Museum

49. *Waiting*, c.1963,
clay print,
44.5 x 50.8 cm, (by conversion),
Exhibited: National Gallery of Canada Biennial, 1965;
Vincent Price Gallery, Chicago, 1967; Marion Nicoll:
A Retrospective, Edmonton and Calgary, 1975,
Courtesy of Masters Gallery Limited

50. *Northern Nesting Grounds*, 1964,
clay print,
35.6 x 44.9 cm, (image),
Exhibited: Alberta Society of Artists
exhibition, 1964/1965;
Vincent Price Gallery, Chicago, 1967,
Collection of the Alberta Art Foundation

51. *Maybe Tomorrow*, 1965,
clay print,
50.8 x 64.8 cm, (by conversion),
Exhibited: "Focus", Edmonton, 1963;
Allied Arts Centre, Calgary, 1963;
Vincent Price Gallery, Chicago, 1967,
Collection of Mrs. Eileen Taylor

52. *Annunciation*, 1965,
clay print,
41.0 x 47.0 cm,
Exhibited: Vincent Price Gallery, Chicago, 1967;
Marion Nicoll: A Retrospective,
Edmonton and Calgary, 1975,
Collection of Shell Canada Limited

53. *Long Prairie Winter*, 1965,
mud print,
46.4 x 61.0 cm,
Exhibited: Red River Exhibition, Winnipeg, 1965;
Vincent Price Gallery, Chicago, 1967,
The Edmonton Art Gallery Collection,
gift of The Alberta Art Foundation, 1984

54. *La Paz*, 1966,
clay print,
41.9 x 50.8 cm,
The Edmonton Art Gallery Collection,
gift of the Alberta Art Foundation, 1984

55. *Red Rock, Black Rock*, 1967,
cardboard print,
40.6 x 50.8 cm,
Art Gallery of Windsor Collection,
gift of the Director's Fund, 1967

56. *Sundogs*, c.1967,
clay print,
41.6 x 46.9 cm, (by conversion),
Courtesy of Masters Gallery Limited

57. *Foothills*, 1968,
clay print,
41.7 x 35.8 cm, (image),
Collection of the Winnipeg Art Gallery,
Acquired with funds from the Winnipeg Foundation

58. *Prairie Farm*, 1970,
collograph,
28 x 48.3 cm (image),
Collection of the Alberta Art Foundation

59. *Birth of a Legend*, 1971,
clay print,
45.5 x 60.5 cm,
The Edmonton Art Gallery Collection,
anonymous donation, 1979

60. *Runes "B"*, 1972,
cardboard print,
60.0 x 55.0 cm,
Collecton of the Edmonton Art Gallery,
gift of the Alberta Art Foundation

61. *Alarum*, 1976,
clay print,
36.8 x 48.9 cm, (by conversion),
Courtesy of Masters Gallery Limited

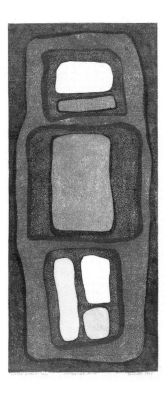

62. *Indian I*, c.1977,
clay print,
19.7 x 45.7 cm, (by conversion),
Courtesy of Masters Gallery Limited

63. *Indian II*, c.1977,
clay print,
14.9 x 45.7 cm, (by conversion),
Courtesy of Masters Gallery Limited

64. *Indian III*, c.1977,
clay print,
26.7 x 45.7 cm, (by conversion),
Courtesy of Masters Gallery Limited

65. *Untitled*, no date,
clay print,
32 x 27.5 cm, (image),
Collection of the Alberta Art Foundation

66. *Untitled*, no date,
clay print,
25.4 x 34.3 cm, (image),
Collection of the Alberta Art Foundation

67. *Standing Figure*, no date,
woodcut,
40.0 x 12.0 cm, (image),
Collection of the Alberta Art Foundation

# Drawings and Sketchbooks

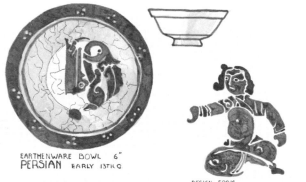

EARTHENWARE BOWL 6"
PERSIAN EARLY 13TH.C

DESIGN FROM
PERSIAN BOWL EARLY 13TH. C.

68. *Sketchbook*, 1937-1938,
mixed media,
14.3 x 23.7 cm, (27 sheets),
Collection of the Glenbow Museum,
gift of Mr. Peter Ohler,
Masters Gallery Limited

69. **Sketchbook**, 1937-1938,
pencil on paper,
12.7 x 17.6 cm, (24 sheets),
Collection of the Glenbow Museum,
gift of Mr. Peter Ohler,
Masters Gallery Limited

70. **On the Ghost**, 1941,
pencil on paper,
11.5 x 15 cm, (image) V,
11.3 x 13 cm, (image) R,
Collection of the Alberta Art Foundation

71. **Sketchbook**, c.1959,
mixed media,
20.4 x 13.0 cm,
Collection of the Glenbow Museum,
gift of Mr. Peter Ohler,
Masters Gallery Limited

72. **Sketchbook**, 1960s,
mixed media,
16.0 x 24.0 cm, (17 sheets),
Collection of the Glenbow Museum,
gift of Mr. Peter Ohler,
Masters Gallery Limited

73. **Red Spring**, 1961,
felt pen and ink,
11.5 x 9.7 cm, (image),
Collection of the Alberta Art Foundation

74. **Trees**, 1965 and 1968,
pencil on paper,
two sheets in single mat, 13 x 23 cm, 18 x 14 cm,
Collection of Chevron Canada Resources Limited

75. **Drawing No. 1**, 1974,
automatic drawing,
ink on paper,
30.5 x 40.5 cm,
Collection of the Alberta Art Foundation

76. **Untitled**, 1978,
automatic drawing,
ink on paper,
35.5 x 28 cm,
Collection of the Alberta Art Foundation

77. **Untitled**, no date,
contour drawing,
pencil on paper,
45.5 x 30.5 cm,
Collection of the Alberta Art Foundation

78. **Untitled**, no date,
contour drawing,
pencil on paper,
45.5 x 30.5 cm,
Collection of the Alberta Art Foundation

79. **Prophet**, no date,
preparatory drawing,
pencil on paper,
13.3 x 10.8 cm, (by conversion),
Collection of Shirley and Peter Savage

80. **Drumheller**, no date,
pencil,
32.0 x 39.5 cm,
Collection of the Alberta Art Foundation

81. **November Sun**, no date,
coloured crayon and pencil,
31.3 x 23.6 cm, (image),
Collection of the Alberta Art Foundation

82. **Untitled**, no date,
pencil on paper,
45.0 x 39.5 cm,
Collection of the Alberta Art Foundation

83. **Friendly Encounter**, no date,
mixed media,
20.3 x 31.6 cm,
Collection of the Alberta Art Foundation

84. **Sketchbook**, no date,
pencil on paper,
21.5 x 28.0 cm, (50 sheets),
Collection of the Glenbow Museum,
gift of Mr. Peter Ohler,
Masters Gallery Limited

85. **Sketchbook**, no date,
mixed media,
23.0 x 30.0 cm, (11 sheets),
Collection of the Glenbow Museum,
gift of Mr. Peter Ohler,
Masters Gallery Limited

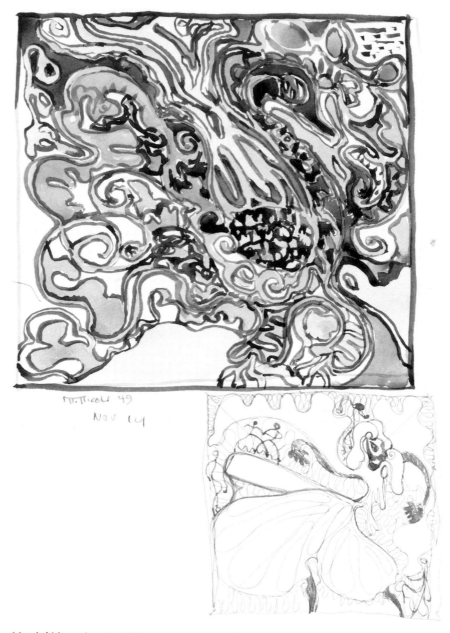

*Untitled* November 14, 1948, automatic watercolour.
Cat. no. 38

# Major Exhibitions and Collections

## Solo Exhibitions

Memorial Exhibition, Glenbow Museum, Calgary, 1985
Masters Gallery, Calgary, 1978
Edmonton Art Gallery and Glenbow Museum, retrospective, 1975
Bonli Gallery, Toronto, 1967
Western Canada Art Circuit, 1966
Yellow Door Gallery, Winnipeg, 1964
Upstairs Gallery, Toronto, 1961 and 1963
Focus Gallery, Edmonton, 1962, 1963, 1964
Bowness Recreation Centre, 1961
Bowness Town Hall, 1960 and 1965
Alberta College of Art, 1959

## Group Exhibitions

Contemporary Art from the Permanent Collection, Glenbow Museum, 1985
New Acquisitions, Glenbow Museum, 1984
Winnipeg West, travelling exhibition, organized by the Edmonton Art Gallery, 1983
Muttart Gallery, Calgary, and Centennial Library, Edmonton, 1979
Albertawork, Calgary, 1977
Graphex, Brantford, Ontario, 1977
Alberta Art Foundation Travelling Exhibition, (Europe, United States and Canada), 1977
Retrospective Print Show, Edmonton, 1973
University of Calgary, 1972
Glenbow Museum, Calgary, 1971
Printmakers Showcase, London, Ontario, 1969
Sear's Vincent Price Gallery, Chicago, 1968
Winnipeg Biennial, 1966
Red River Exhibition, Winnipeg, 1965
National Gallery of Canada, 5th, 6th, and 7th Biennials of Canadian Painting, Ottawa, 1963, 1965, 1968
Toronto Arts Festival, 1962
Allied Art Centre, 1960, 1963 and 1965
Alberta Society of Artists exhibitions 1949, c.1950, 1954, 1957, 1960, 1962, 1964/1965, and 1966
Regular contributor to Canadian Society of Painters in Watercolour,

## Major Collections

Marion Nicoll's prints, watercolours, drawings and paintings are included in the following collections:

Alberta Art Foundation, Edmonton
Edmonton Art Gallery, Edmonton
Calgary Centre for the Performing Arts, Calgary
Winnipeg Art Gallery, Winnipeg
Art Gallery of Windsor, Windsor, Ont.
London Regional Art Gallery, London, Ont.
National Gallery of Canada, Ottawa
Art Gallery of Hamilton, Hamilton, Ont.
The Art Gallery of Memorial University, St. John's, Nfld.
Alberta House, London, England
University of Calgary, Calgary
Southern Alberta Institute of Technology, Calgary
Alberta College of Art , Calgary
University of Lethbridge Art Gallery, Lethbridge
University of Alberta, Edmonton
Glenbow Museum, Calgary
The Whyte Museum of the Canadian Rockies, Banff
Leighton Foundation, Midnapore
Kresge's International Collection, Detroit
The CIL Collection, Montreal
Shell Canada Collection, Calgary
Esso Collection, Calgary
Petro-Canada Collection, Calgary
Chevron Resources Collection, Calgary
The Government of Alberta, Edmonton.

# Lenders to the Exhibition

The Alberta Art Foundation
The Edmonton Art Gallery
The Art Gallery of Hamilton
The Leighton Foundation
The London Regional Art Gallery
Nickle Arts Museum, University of Calgary
Ringhouse Gallery, University of Alberta
The University of Lethbridge Art Gallery
The Art Gallery of Windsor
The Winnipeg Art Gallery
Chevron Canada Resources Limited
Gulf Canada Oil Limited
Petro-Canada Art Collection
Shell Canada Limited
Masters Gallery Limited
Mrs. Betty Anne Graves
Mr. and Mrs. Pierre Hetu
Mrs. Moani Moss
Gerald Pencer
Shirley and Peter Savage
Joan and Dale Simmons
Mrs. Eileen Taylor
E.D.D. Tavender Collection
Anonymous lenders.

# Photographic Credits

Cover and pages 6, 9, 11, 13 (lower), 16, 17, 20, 21 (left), 22, 23, 24, 25, 27, 28, 31 (upper), 32 (upper), 33, 34, 42, 45, 57, 58, 59 (left), 60, 61, 62, 63, 64, and 66, Ron Marsh, Glenbow Museum;

pages 29, 39 (upper), and 49, E. Lazare, courtesy of the Edmonton Art Gallery;

pages 10, 30, 31 (lower), page 32 (lower), 37, 41, 43, 44, 59 (right), courtesy of the Alberta Art Foundation;

pages 13 (upper), 15, courtesy of the Art Gallery of Ontario;

page 39 (lower), courtesy of the London Regional Art Gallery;

pages 14, 38, and 40, courtesy of the Nickle Arts Museum, University of Calgary;

page 21 (right), courtesy of the Whitney Museum of American Art;

page 56, courtesy of the University of Lethbridge Art Gallery;

biographical photographs courtesy of the Glenbow Photographic Archives.

Sketchbook drawing (Mountain Scene), no date.
Cat. no. 85

# Credits

Design: Eugene Ouchi, Stepstone Design
Editor: Beth Duthie
Typesetting: Walford and Foy, Calgary
Printing: Phoenix Press Limited, Calgary
Binding: Atlas Trade Bindery, Edmonton